FINDING A
SPIRITUAL FRIEND

And though one might prevail against another, two will withstand one. A threefold cord is not quickly broken.
—Ecclesiastes 4:12

FINDING
A SPIRITUAL
FRIEND

How Friends and Mentors
Can Make Your Faith Grow

TIMOTHY JONES

UPPER
ROOM BOOKS
NASHVILLE

Fininding a Spiritual Friend

Library of Congress Cataloging-in-Publication Data

Jones, Timothy K., 1955-
    Finding a spiritual friend : how friends and mentors can make your
faith grow / by Timothy Jones.
        p.   cm.
    Includes bibliographical references.
    ISBN 0-8358-0857-2
    1. Friendship—Religious aspects—Christianity.   I. Title.
BV4647.F7J65   1998
248.4'6—dc21   98-38840
                                                                   CIP

Printed in the United States of America

To Kevin Miller

CONTENTS

ACKNOWLEDGMENTS

This book owes its existence to a host of mentors and friends who through the years have modeled what I tried to capture on the printed page.

Thanks are due to several who helped during the writing: Kevin Miller, who gave not only great feedback but also prayer support and friendship, and the writers' group at Church of the Resurrection in West Chicago, Illinois. Thanks go also to Janice Grana, JoAnn Miller, Rita Collett, and Karen Williams at Upper Room Books for helpful suggestions.

FOREWORD

$\mathcal{Y}$ou have in your hands a marvelous resource to assist you in your spiritual journey. Timothy Jones knows firsthand the importance of a spiritual friend. His own experience prepares him to help find the way toward life-giving relationships with other Christians. Timothy not only provides a clear and concise road map for the person seeking a spiritual friend or mentor, but he helps us identify the reasons we need one and the rewards of having one.

For more than twenty years, I have been leading retreats for people seeking a deeper walk with Jesus Christ. It is always disturbing to know that after the retreat experience many will go to their homes without the help that spiritual companionship can provide. Without that support and accountability they will quickly lose much of the transforming benefit of a time apart. Now there is a resource that I can confidently put into the hands of every seeker and know that if they follow the suggestions here they will be able to establish and maintain a transforming relationship with other Christians.

One of the beautiful and important aspects of this resource is that it lets the seeking reader walk with the experienced author who has already traveled this path and knows the way with all its risks and all its rewards. *Finding a Spiritual Friend: How Friends and Mentors Can Make Your Faith Grow* is a practical, down-to-earth and honest account of how one goes about finding a person who can become a spiritual friend. It then offers clear suggestions about how that friendship can be sustained for transformation for both parties. Because the author has walked this path attentively, learning from his own experience, and has shared experiences with countless contemporary Christians, and has read and lived with the saints of the past, he is able to give clear and wise direction to the reader.

The author provides helpful response to the simple and profound questions that arise when two or more people determine to help each other walk faithfully with God in all of life. How does one find a spiritual friend in today's world? How can Christians help each other to grow in their relationship with God? What are some of the risks to be considered? What are some danger points to be avoided? How can spiritual friendship be nurtured and sustained for a lifetime? Can spiritual friendships be appropriately ended? What can I expect from spiritual friendship? Can I be a spiritual friend for my spiritual friend?

All these questions and more have been confronted, carefully considered, and wisely answered in this creative guide for persons serious about their spiritual journey. I commend it highly to every seeker and especially to every person giving spiritual direction, leading retreats, and giving guidance to the spiritual growth of others. Pastors and persons training others for pastoral ministry will find a trustworthy resource to enhance and enable ministry of spiritual care.

In this book, the wisdom of the centuries is added to contemporary experience to provide a sound foundation for the experienced traveler and the hesitant beginner on the spiritual journey. There is enough depth here to challenge the serious seeker in understanding the theological and psychological undergirding of spiritual friendship. But the style and content is readily accessible to every reader. The depth and scope of the work has not overlooked the nuts and bolts of making the concept of spiritual friendship understandable and workable in the average life and the average setting. It is a resource that I will return to for personal guidance and one that I will recommend to others. ⌁

Reuben P. Job

ONE

The Friend We Can't Do Without

No one can walk without a guide.

Augustine

Two are better than one . . .

Ecclesiastes 4:9

ᕇ

*O*ne autumn ten years ago I admitted to myself that I was not doing well when it came to friends.

I had moved to a suburb of Chicago to begin a new career. My wife and children and I knew almost no one. We lived in a cramped apartment and we struggled with scant success to stretch my entry-level editor's salary to make ends meet. For all my love of my new career, the stress of our move was compounded by my having to learn the ropes of full-time professional editing, something I had done only as an earnest amateur.

I also soon realized I was lonely. While church and work and neighbors gave me regular contact with dozens of people, while I had parents and in-laws and aunts and uncles who cared for me, to say nothing of a loving wife, I still longed for someone with whom to go deeper. I needed a soul friend. I wanted to make friendship more than haphazard. I realized it deserved more than emotional leftovers or chance encounters. That's when I turned to Kevin, a colleague at my work, and, as you will see in pages to come, a profound help in my spiritual life.

When you stop to think about it, none of us is wise enough or strong enough or clear-eyed enough to live well without the presence and help of others. We are not made to navigate the challenges of life and love and faith solo. No person "is an island, entire of itself" wrote the poet John Donne; every person is "a piece of the continent, a part of the main."[1] Solitude has its place, but we are made to live with and learn from others.

Of course, a part of us still admires the self-made person who by grit and talent and inner strength accomplishes great things. We secretly like the sound of the song that declares, "I did it my way." But when we opt always to take on life's challenges by ourselves, we forget how much others can enrich our lives—or perhaps save our sanity. Even when no crisis looms or no deep emotional scars need healing, we need companions, friends, helpers. It may be as simple as wanting someone to go with us to a movie. Or as profound as needing to confess a failing that shames us. No wonder that pollster Daniel Yankelovich found that seventy percent of Americans say they have few close friends (though many acquaintances), and that they experience this as a void in their lives. We spend time with dozens of people but learn from their lives only haphazardly. We have fishing or tennis buddies. Colleagues at work. Neighbors we greet with a wave and smile. Yet only occasionally do we go deep in talking about our sorrows and dreams.

That certainly holds true for the spiritual life.

All around us an unprecedented spiritual awakening is taking hold. When polled, an overwhelming majority of people claim to pray. People of every walk of life evidence a great and growing spiritual hunger. But along with the interest comes what a friend of mine calls "spiritual loneliness." All the spiritual curiosity in the world cannot compensate for the need for spiritual guidance. We long for soul friends. We want help for the questions that any spiritually healthy life must face: How do I pray? Will I know when God speaks? Is God calling me in a new vocational direction? We have to admit we don't have a fund of wisdom for every step of the way.

When it comes to our innermost selves, the spiritual dimension, we need what only others can bring.

That realization doesn't always come easily, of course. We prefer to cultivate an image (and self-image) of sufficiency. When we are around other spiritually minded people, a friend of mine likes to say, we share only "the highlights" and keep quiet about the "lowlights." We grow vaguely uneasy if we must turn to another. We may even subtly, subconsciously believe that only the spiritually weak or wimpy need help. But it does not take long to see the hollowness of such an approach. We long for companions for the spiritual life—whether they be prayer partners, spiritual mentors, simple friends, or small-group members.

This book is predicated on the assumption that the Christian life should not—cannot—be lived in lonely isolation. Faith is no do-it-yourself project. When it comes to our innermost selves, the spiritual dimension, we need what only others can bring. Imperfect as any friendship or mentoring relationship must be, we will not go far if we don't enjoy something like it. We need others with whom we can talk and pray. Without relationships that bring spiritual nurture, our lives with God will suffer.

I am talking here about more than the superficial contacts so typical of our relating. Coffee hours or fellowship suppers at church, by themselves, won't lead to the kind of personal interaction that can really help us. I once heard about a congregation in which the church board's stock response to couples with hurting marriages was to deliver tapes of the pastor's sermons on biblical marriage. But more than insight delivered at a distance is needed. In so many areas of life what matters most is a personal touch, a "walking with" in the gritty work of establishing new patterns, leaving behind old dysfunctions, and opening more fully to God. For all the theological books, religious radio programs, and Sunday morning services we enjoy, many of us are starved for one-on-one support and accountability.

I want to suggest, then, that every believer can benefit from a friend or mentor, a confidant or prayer partner, with whom he or she can freely discuss the trials and triumphs of living for and with God. Such a relationship need not be elaborate or out of reach of the ordinary Christian. If you have ever been intimidated by those who speak of having a "spiritual director," you need not worry. If you envision needing to hand over hours out of every week, let me set you at ease. What I propose about finding a spiritual friend or mentor (and I'll explain the difference) can happen naturally and simply.

But it can make a huge difference.

I believe a friend in the Spirit may give us the support that can encourage us to be more disciplined in prayer or more confident in the love of God. Indeed, our lack of steady progress in the Christian life may be pointing us finally to the futility of trying on our own. "If two lie together, they keep warm; but how can one keep warm alone?" (Eccles. 4:11). Our frustrations only point us toward the value of a friendship or accountability relationship that will help us stay spiritually "warm." We know—and God knows—that we cannot do without others. Surely this is why one of the important words in the New Testament is the word *koinonia*, translated into English as "communion," "fellowship," "partnership," "intimacy," "participation," "sharing in common," or "giving to one another." Fellowship of this sort means giving and receiving, and not on a superficial level. Without it, our Christian growth will be stunted.

A man I'll call Chuck is a good example. He is in his thirties, accomplished in his job, a single parent, a faithful churchgoer. But when asked if men like him tend to have true friends, he noted, "I have a lot of acquaintances, and I've been in some wonderful Bible study groups, but as far as a close friend or a one-on-one relationship, no. It's been a struggle. I need something like that, but it's uncharted water to me."

Or I think of a friend I'll call Margaret. She is eager to grow in her relationship with God but finds that weekly worship cannot satisfy all her questions or provide all the support she needs. She has questions about how God speaks to people today—indeed, if she has heard God's voice at all when she prays. Her church friends mean well but do not always feel equipped to address her specific concerns. Margaret lives some hours away from us, and when my wife and I visited her and her husband for a weekend, Margaret and my wife stayed up into the wee hours. Margaret was like a sponge—dry, eager to soak up any moisture from another Christian who could come alongside and provide loving counsel.

In my own life, my search for friendship and help has found expression in a variety of helpful—sometimes life-changing—relationships. In the churches I first served as pastor, for example, Bill, Earl, and other older pastors helped me apply all I learned from seminary textbooks. As a young pastor, I met monthly over pizza with David, a neighboring pastor. He became my friend and confidant. I even went for a time to a professional "spiritual director." Up until a recent move, I met with Kevin, a friend and work colleague, once a week. Our friendship became the fruit of my restless reaching out described earlier. After I had gotten to know Kevin at the office, I suggested, with some trepidation, that we meet regularly to offer mutual support and prayer. We decided to give it a try and meet once a week.

For five years thereafter, Kevin and I took a lunch hour

once a week to share our stresses, anxieties, joys, even doubts. Usually we simply shut the door and met in his office at the magazine where he works as editor. We gave encouragement, prodded the other to new ways of thinking, and always prayed aloud for each other. Mostly we helped each other listen to what God was saying through the raw material of our lives' routines and milestones.

The influence of Kevin and all the rest lives in me in lasting and sometimes hidden ways, and my experiences with these prayer partners and spiritual mentors—the things I've learned and things I'd do differently if I had it to do over—will feature prominently in the pages that follow.

All around us—in churches, office buildings, Bible study groups, neighborhoods—are people who can help us in our Christian growth. They need not be theological experts or spiritual geniuses, nor must we be such to help others in turn. All we need to begin is a willingness to try.

A FRIEND IN THE SPIRIT

If you think this is some innovation, an experiment for the spiritually trendy or adventurous, think again. Having a spiritual friend or mentor is instead a practice with long precedent in the Bible and Christian history. The church has thrived for centuries because of it. Spiritual friendship, in other words, is something we need to recover.

The Bible supports this. Jesus sent out his seventy followers in twos (Luke 10:1). He knew that we cannot face the battles of faithfulness alone. And he said, "For where two or three are gathered in my name, I am there among them" (Matt. 18:20). So much for radical individualism! From Elijah and Elisha in the Hebrew scriptures to Mary and Elizabeth in the New Testament, we see God using mentors and friends in the lives of God's people.

Paul the apostle exemplified this. He knew how important others can be in our faith journey. To the church at Corinth he wrote, "I appeal to you, then, be imitators of me. For this reason I sent you Timothy, who is my beloved and faithful child in the Lord, to remind you of my ways in Christ Jesus" (1 Cor. 4:16-17). Paul befriended and "mentored" Timothy and in turn sent Timothy to do the same to the Corinthians. We can imagine how important this mentoring, modeling, and support was for Paul's younger charge (see "Young Timothy's Secret" on page 26) and for the whole body of believers at Corinth. Examples from the scriptures abound, as we will see.

As new generations came on the stage of what God was doing in the church, the practice never died. Consider this random assortment of what church history "greats" had to say about how much we need spiritual helpers:

• Augustine, a great leader in the fourth-century church, emphasized that "no one can walk without a guide."

• Isaac the Syrian in the late sixth century urged, "Confide your thoughts to a man who, though he lack learning, has studied the work [of prayer] in practice."

• Bernard of Clairvaux (1090–1153) argued, "He becomes the disciple of a fool who sets up to be his own teacher."

• The twelfth-century English monk Aelred of Rievaulx said, "Friendship is like a step to raise us to the love and knowledge of God."

• Martin Luther (sixteenth century reformer) made it a habit to exercise a ministry of spiritual guidance by personal presence and by letter. In an early letter to a fellow student, Luther urged his friend to reveal "the condition of thy soul."

• Teresa of Avila (sixteenth century) said, "It is a great advantage for us to be able to consult someone who knows us, so that we may learn to know ourselves."

• The great seventeenth-century Puritan Richard Baxter

argued that the one entrusted with the care of another must not "slightly slubber over" the ministry of personal counsel, even—especially—with the "strong."

• And John Wesley, founder of Methodism, wrote in his *Plain Account of Christian Perfection,* "So you ascribe all the knowledge you have to God, and in this respect you are humble. But if you think you have more than you really have; or if you think you are so taught of God, as not longer to need [another person's] teaching, pride lies at the door."

---

*Teresa of Avila said,
"It is a great advantage for us to be
able to consult someone
who knows us, so that we may
learn to know ourselves."*

The testimony of the church's great leaders and teachers is clear.

In our own day, centers for training spiritual directors are springing up all over the world. Churches have started formal mentoring programs for youth or adults. Scores of articles on spiritual friendship and direction have been published in the last decades. Books with titles such as *Soul Friend* and *Spiritual Friend* have become favorites among the spiritually seeking. The idea of spiritual direction and friendship, concludes Richard J. Foster, "is highly applicable to the contemporary scene. It is a beautiful expression of divine guidance through the help of our brothers and sisters."[2]

Many names identify this special relationship: spiritual direction, spiritual friendship, discipling, mentoring. Some writers use the terms *spiritual companion* or *soul friend* (an old Irish tradition). My friend David Mains uses the term prayer partner.[3] As this variety suggests, the relationship we explore in this book can take more than one form, from a clear mentoring relationship to a more mutual peer arrangement. Later we will explore the dynamics of both mentoring and more informal friendships. As we will see, both, and even a combination, have their place.

COMPANIONS FOR THE SOUL'S ITINERARY

All this may suggest that you have been doing without something with great potential for your spiritual growth. Or you may already have discovered that your relationship with God bears great fruit only when it is rooted in relationships with others, and you want to learn more.

Wherever you find yourself, the options are wide open. You might benefit, for example, from simple weekly meetings like my friends Susan and Virginia enjoy; these two young women meet over their lunch hours to talk, listen together to God, and pray for the week's special needs and joys. Or you may be like one man who was wrestling with a persistent temptation. He said to his friend, "When we see each other every week, ask me, 'How are you doing with that temptation?' " Or you may want to approach a sage person whose depth and spiritual maturity might make all the difference in your own growth in faith. As you will soon see, a number of possibilities await.

It may take effort. You may need to be intentional. Writer Eugene H. Peterson at first had trouble finding "experienced companions in the soul's itinerary," but his longing for direction and companionship wouldn't go away: "And then I began to find them, one by one, here and there, in obscure corners of libraries far from the bestseller racks. In quiet, easy-to-overlook persons well out of the promotional limelight. . . . They were dealing with the questions that I raised whenever I was moving into the heart of the faith, struggling to find my personal way through the difficulties of Scripture or the mysteries of prayer or the 'dark night of the soul.'"[4] It may simply require perseverance.

The one-on-one arrangement we accent here may not be for everyone, or at least not for all the time. While all can benefit from being accountable to another and having others listen and pray for them, this can happen in a small group. It can happen very informally. It certainly happens between many spouses. Still, there is value in involving one other person—a soul friend or spiritual mentor—in our Christian growth.

Inviting someone to help us grow in faith is no panacea, of course. As in any relationship, tensions can arise. Or an unhealthy exclusivism may creep in. But the companionship we seek, and sometimes ourselves give to others, holds the promise of making our Christian lives richer and more satisfying. This book just may help if your Christian life seems stale or stalled. It may finally convince you of what you already suspect, that a friend or mentor or spiritual helper can make your Christian life more fruitful. The pages that follow will provide the insights and the steps you need to find help from another, and in turn give to another.

FOR FURTHER REFLECTION

• Read Philippians 3:17. When Paul tells the Philippians to "observe those who live according to the example you have in us," what do you think he meant? What does that say about the importance of truth's being not only taught but "caught"?

• One woman explained the value of friendship, "We're not meant to be alone. We're meant to support one another, to be like trees in a forest whose roots intertwine and hold each other up." To what extent is she right? What does that have to do with finding a spiritual mentor or friend?

• Think back to times when a friend or teacher helped you understand something about yourself. How did the insight help you gain a new perspective? take a new step of faith? better understand your doubts or questions? enable you to endure a trying situation?

• What are the limitations of the "rugged individualism" that seems so much a part of the atmosphere of our culture and of some churches? In what specific areas in your life would you benefit from a spiritual helper and friend?

• Ask acquaintances or family members to tell you about influential people in their lives. If necessary, gently probe to find out how your friends' values can be traced to others' mentoring and modeling. Write down here what you discovered.

_____

_____

_____

_____

_____

_____

_____

_____

_____

YOUNG TIMOTHY'S SECRET

When Paul the apostle told the church at Philippi to "join with *others* in following my example" (Phil. 3:17, NIV, italics mine), one of the *others* he may well have had in mind was his younger colleague Timothy, whose name surfaces throughout the New Testament. Timothy and Paul's relationship was a classic case of spiritual mentoring and friendship. What they shared may explain Timothy's remarkable influence in the early church.

Paul was not the only one to have a hand in shaping Timothy's faith, of course. Paul notes that Timothy's grandmother Lois and mother, Eunice, had a role in the young man's coming to faith (2 Tim. 1:5). But Paul still claims a special place. He calls Timothy his "loyal child in the faith" (1 Tim. 1:2) and his "beloved child" (2 Tim. 1:2).

Much of Paul's influence seems to have worn off on Timothy "on the job." Paul took Timothy along on his preaching missions, and they together "went from town to town" so that "the churches were strengthened in the faith and increased in numbers daily" (Acts 16:5). In Philippians, Paul notes, "Like a son with a father he has served with me in the work of the gospel" (2:22). And Paul lists Timothy as a cowriter in his first and second letters to the Thessalonians.

Such partnership in ministry no doubt strengthened Timothy's own faith.

We can only surmise the details of how they spent time together working, talking, praying, keeping each other accountable; but it is clear that they did. Paul took a tender, personal concern in his younger friend, as we see in his worries over Timothy's health in 1 Timothy 5:23: "No longer drink only water, but take a little wine for the sake of your stomach and your frequent ailments." And while Paul respected Timothy and counted him a colleague, he was unafraid to challenge him to continued growth. "I remind you," Paul wrote to Timothy, "to rekindle the gift of God that is within you through the laying on of my hands" (2 Tim. 1:6). That personal touch must have had more power to shape Timothy's life than a host of sermons. ᓚ

TWO

What to Expect

*Behind every saint stands another saint. That is the great
tradition. I never learnt anything myself by my own nose.*
Baron Friedrich von Hügel[1]

*Iron sharpens iron,
and one person sharpens the wits of another.*
Proverbs 27:17

◠

When I first began meeting with Kevin for conversation and prayer, I wasn't sure what to expect. I
knew that sometimes I wanted someone to talk to about the
things that excited or disappointed me. I knew that I longed
for more support for my efforts to live a spiritual life. I also
knew how often I walked through daily circumstances only
partly aware of what was happening, only dimly seeing
God's hand in everyday turns of events. I suspected a companion in the Spirit could listen and pray with me. Could
help me see something I would otherwise miss.

And I was right.

Aelred of Rievaulx, a twelfth-century English monk
and writer, discovered this. He penned a testimony to
friendship that still moves readers today. "A [person] is to

be compared to a beast," he wrote, "if he [or she] has no one to rejoice with . . . in adversity, no one to whom to unburden his [or her] mind if any annoyance crosses his [or her] path or with whom to share some unusually sublime or illuminating inspiration. . . . [That person] is entirely alone who is without a friend. But, " said Aelred, "what happiness, what security, what joy to have someone to whom you dare to speak on terms of equality . . . one to whom you need have no fear to confess your failings; one to whom you can unblushingly make known what progress you have made in the spiritual life!"[2]

No less so in the twentieth century, a partner in spiritual growth can benefit us in a number of striking and lasting ways. Here are several.

FINDING GOD IN EVERYDAY LIFE

A spiritual friend or mentor can assist us in understanding the deepr significance of what happens to us. I am sometimes prone to think that my daily conversations at the office or my worries about next month's bills have little to do with my spiritual life, but I have come to see instead that God constantly is at work in my life—in the dramatic and the ordinary. All life is grist for prayerful, thoughtful conversation.

While many of us look for God in crises and milestones, a guide can help us find God in the everyday. He or she does so not by freely giving advice but by prayerfully helping us see the significance of our lives' events, by helping us grasp how God is speaking and leading through the ordinary turns and straight stretches.

"[It may be simply] taking your children to school and kissing your wife good-bye," writes novelist and minister Frederick Buechner. "Eating lunch with a friend. Trying to do a decent day's work . . . There is no event so commonplace but that God is present within it, always hiddenly, always leaving you room to recognize him or not recognize him, but all the more fascinatingly because of that, all the more compellingly and hauntingly."[3]

Sometimes, though, I need help in seeing God's hand in the ordinary turns. More than once Kevin provided a sounding board when I considered a job change. When someone hurt me and left me confused, unsure how to respond, Kevin helped me sort through what was legitmate criticism and what was insensitive understanding of who I was. Later I saw strokes slowly ravage my mother's ability to function. Kevin listened patiently to my concerns and helped me find divine resources to cope with the grief and anxiety.

Aelred of Rievaulx, a twelfth-century English monk and writer, wrote, "What happiness, what security, what joy to have someone to whom you dare to speak on terms of equality . . . one to whom you need have no fear to confess your failings; one to whom you can unblushingly make known what progress you have made in the spiritual life!"

I've done a similar thing for Kevin. At one point he was asking himself if he should consider ordained ministry. One night he had a jolting dream where he found himself a low-paid errand boy in a luxury resort. He awakened convinced the frightening dream was picturing his life as pastor in his largely well-to-do denomination. When he shared it with me, I helped him put it in perspective. As he told me:

> I was very surprised when you said, "Don't let the dream and discouragement make you write off the whole concept of serving in the church." That response came out of the fact that for three years you've heard these pastoral longings coming out of me. Even if my longings don't get expressed in an ordained way, you told me, "That's a part of you, so don't just throw it out," even though I was ready to. You saw my deepest heart better than I did. I don't think someone who had only known me for three weeks could have ever said that.

I know a woman who has found, as she says, "someone who is always there for me. I may go for a month at a time without getting together with her, but I know that I can call her and she'll understand. She can hear my heated feelings about a situation and help me think it through in a logical manner or give me biblical principles. Sometimes she'll mention a book she's reading. She has a way of laying things out so I can solve problems on my own."

A spiritual friend gives you another set of eyes. He or she may see something when your own vision gets cloudy.

THE PRESENTS OF PRESENCE

A spiritual friend supports with simple presence. When Kevin and I began meeting, we knew that neither one of us had a degree in spiritual direction or a license in counseling. Not only does that not matter, such trappings sometimes get in the way. We found that week in, week out, we gave each other something more important than professional advice: support. We fulfilled weekly the charge of Paul to the church at Galatia, "Bear one another's burdens, and in this way you will fulfill the law of Christ"

(6:2). We helped each other face life's traumas and trials with the assurance that another knows about and brings to the Lord the week's hurts and hopes.

It's no wonder pollster George Gallup has found that three out of ten Americans are involved in some kind of small group and that another one in ten wishes he or she were. I know that in many groups much goes on: Bible study, book discussions, recovery work. But I believe much of their appeal also has to do with our fundamental need to be with others. The presence of another (or others) makes a huge difference.

Once when I was passed up for a promotion and saw it given to another colleague, Kevin's friendsdhip became a source of wonderful comfort. During calmer, more stable times in my life, it has meant a great deal to know that someone will be present with me while I reflect out loud on my week's dry times and hallowed moments. Here's how Kevin articulated an instance when my simple presence mattered to him:

> After I got back from my dad's funeral, and another two weeks or so had gone by, the immediate expressions of sympathy from people in the office—the cards and phone calls—became a trickle. I realized that for the majority of the people I know, my father's death was over and done with. I had this tremendous fear that here I was just coming out of the initial shock and entering my true grief work, and all of a sudden nobody was around to help me with it. But I remember thinking to myself, *I know Tim will listen to me. If I need to bring this up, I can talk about it with him.* I had a safe place to bring up whatever I was working on.

I am fascinated by research that shows that unburdening ourselves of painful memories or guilty secrets may significantly improve our physical health. Researcher James W. Pennebaker found that "confronting our deepest thoughts and feelings can have remarkable short- and long-term health benefits." Pennebaker charted measurable physiological differences in people who confessed wrongs or talked about disturbing personal episodes compared with those who kept their secrets locked inside. The difference seemed related not so much to any specific counsel given in response but rather to the *simple act of bringing into the open what had been hidden.* "There appears to be [within us]," he concluded, "something akin to an urge to confess. Not disclosing our thoughts and feelings can be unhealthy. Divulging them can be healthy."[4]

My own experience with spiritual friends and mentors confirms that what is true with physical health is even truer with my soul. I find freedom in being able to tell someone of my failings and be reminded of God's forgiving, renewing grace in Christ. It means a great deal to know I do not carry these things on my own. The forgiveness comes from God, but God does not hesitate to use human agents sometimes to keep me from losing sight of it.

CHARACTER BY CONTAGION

A spiritual friend's insights and character can "rub off" on us. The corporate world has discovered recently what Christians have sometimes missed. In business an executive will often "coach" or "mentor" a junior partner— supervising the younger's decisions or introducing him or her to key business contacts—modeling some of the intangibles of leadership. Coaching and mentoring have become buzzwords in business circles.

Christians too need to draw strength from others, whether the help comes from a peer and friend or a wiser mentor. Many people have influenced my commitment to Christ. And often that influence has come by seeing how they react to a situation, by noticing the choices they make, by observing the ups and downs of daily life.

I like the story Robert Clinton tells about Harold, a fellow church member who persuaded him to join a small group that was to meet for six weeks to help members grow spiritually. One time Robert and Harold traded Bibles for a week. Recounts Robert,

> I saw in the flyleaf the remark, "Started reading the Bible through for the first time," and [Harold] gave a date. Then the remark, "Finished reading the Bible through for the first time," and the date was a year later. This was repeated three times. He had been a Christian for only three years. I was challenged. I had been a nongrowing Christian for about eighteen years and had never once read entirely through my Bible. So I began to read my Bible through systematically for the first time. His Bible was well-marked—underlined, with notations in the margin. I picked up that habit, too.[5]

Character and devotion must sometimes be "caught" as well as taught. "Without examples, without imitation," historian Robert Wilken writes, "there can be no human life or civilization, no art or culture, no virtue or holiness. The elementary activities of . . . learning to speak or sculpting a statue have their beginning in the imitation of what others do." Wilken concludes, "By observing the lives of holy men and women and imitating their deeds we become virtuous. Before we can become doers we must first become spectators."[6] As Paul put it, "Observe those who live according to the example you have in us" (Phil. 3:17), and "Be imitators of me" (1 Cor. 4:16). Sometimes we need to see the Christian life lived out; we need to stand in the presence of the genuine article, not just be told about it.

PRAYING WITH ANOTHER

A spiritual friend can help us tap into the power of shared prayer. "I tell you, if two of you agree on earth about anything you ask, it will be done for you by my Father in heaven" (Matt. 18:19). Praying with another believer has great effect. There seems to be something about two people praying that is greater than the sum total of the individual prayers.

Of course, prayer is never a wand that we wield to get

what we want. But the Bible is clear that we should "pray for one another" because "the prayer of the righteous is powerful and effective" (James 5:16). And when it comes to intercession, the Bible is clear that two are often better than one.

---

*Sometimes we need to **see** the Christian life lived out; we need to stand in the presence of the genuine article, not just be told about it.*

This is not a matter of mere psychological benefits, either, of simply *feeling* better for having the support of another's prayer. Whatever the circumstances we find ourselves in, praying with another person seems to invoke or enlist God's power in a way that solitary prayer cannot. Praying *with* someone, I find my own prayers buttressed and undergirded by another's, and the Holy Spirit uses our joint praying to accomplish much.

Indeed, prayer is indispensable in ensuring that spiritual friendship or mentoring becomes more than mere counseling. My friend Kevin says it this way:

> There have been a lot of times where I've been upset about something stressful in my life. As you've prayed out loud for me, I may not even concentrate on what you're saying. But later that afternoon, I suddenly realize *I'm really feeling better about that situation.* And then I think, *That's right;*

Tim prayed for me. I realize that the prayer aspect of it is extremely valuable.

THE ACCOUNTABILITY CONNECTION

A spiritual partner can help us ground our spiritual life in something more solid than private experience or personal opinion. Failings of prominent Christians hit the news perennially. Whether we are famous or relatively unknown, the need for accountability—for people who can help us avoid error and be true to our best selves—is as great as ever. The temptation to cut corners on what really matters confronts all of us. How spiritual some of my ambitions sometimes seem, how clever my excuses for not doing well appear! Until, that is, a friend sees my mixed motives or my rationalizations—and has the courage to point them out.

Sometimes personal ambition blinds me, for example, to what my daily schedule is costing me in stress. When my commitments crowd out time for exercise or prayer or family relationships, I need someone to remind me that certain "urgent" tasks may not be worth the compromise. It may be more important that I have time to pray or give attention to my children than take on a tempting writing assignment. A friend or mentor can help me balance competing demands and orient my life to the Christian way.

Or a spiritual friend or mentor can help me when I am tempted to give in to feelings of worthlessness. When powerful inner voices (or others' brickbats) condemn me, my friend reminds me that I am still cherished by God. He can build the courage in me that allows me to base my life on something more profound than others' approval. I may become deceived by sin's subtleties, insensitive to its effects. Sometimes I need a prodding voice. Other times an encouraging one. There are areas where I cannot be completely objective. No wonder a proverb says that he who is his own doctor has a fool for a physician.

That is why writer Ben Campbell Johnson was brought up short once when someone asked, "To whom are you accountable?" He proudly responded, "To no one but

God!" But the presumption of that answer began to haunt him, and he soon realized that to think Christians have need for no one else could be a recipe for spiritual disaster. Soon he was searching for a spiritual mentor.[7]

LEARNING TO PRAY

A friend or mentor can help us in the lifelong task of growing in spiritual vitality. Most Christians feel keenly the importance of praying. For all of prayer's importance, however, few of us feel our prayer lives are complete. Most Christians feel they fall far short of Paul's admonition to "pray without ceasing" (1 Thess. 5:17). And who of us doesn't feel that our "practice of the presence of God" could benefit from coaching or encouraging?

Time and again, I have invested a lot of energy in coping with a stressful situation and have told a spiritual friend, only to have him gently ask, "How much time have you spent sitting in God's presence this week?" There's something about that insistent question that keeps me focused on priorities, that reminds me that the goal of life is pleasing and glorifying God.

Meeting regularly with another can help me stay strong in other areas of life that grow out of spiritual vitality, such as sexual purity, financial integrity, and family commitments. A soul friend or mentor can help me keep my eyes on God's expectations for my behavior and God's larger purposes for my life. "If the doors of perception were cleansed," wrote William Blake, "everything would appear as it is, infinite."[8] But my "doors of perception," my customary outlook on daily life, often gets cluttered. I frequently need someone to keep me from missing the "big picture."

A soul friend can encourage us to keep our hearts focused on things of eternal significance, encourage us to make the hard choices, and thereby prepare for living forever in God's presence. Left to myself, it is too easy to forget that "this slight momentary affliction is preparing us for an eternal weight of glory beyond all measure" (2 Cor.

4:17). With a soul friend's help, I will be assisted in living for Christ.

OVERCOMING OUR HESITATIONS

If having a spiritual friend or mentor can have such impact, why don't more of us ensure that it is part of our Christian lives?

Few things frighten some of us more than revealing our inner selves. Men in our culture especially may feel awkward at expressing feelings. They do well "shooting the breeze." But sitting down to explore deeply personal themes?

A person's age may contribute to the hesitations. Sometimes Christians who had their formative years prior to World War II, for example, didn't take in the mood of the share-all sixties and seventies where sensitivity and vulnerability were the watchwords.

We may also fear the risks—What happens if things go sour? Or, as Alan Jones notes, "There is always the danger of the well-meaning or spiritually bossy charging into someone's life uninvited and doing some real damage."[9] We may worry that turning to another will turn into a relationship of unhealthy dependency. Perhaps we fear we do not know anyone who would make the ideal partner.

Our hesitancy may have theological roots. We who cherish the truth that we have one great high priest as our mediator (Heb. 9:15) may fear that turning to others undercuts our dependence on God. Perhaps we subtly distrust any human authority.

Whatever the risks (which we will touch on in later chapters), the benefits of sharing our Christian journey with another outweigh the potential problems. The dangers should make us discerning but not paralyzed.

Of course, those to whom we turn for help must be worthy of our confidence. A guide who in blindness or ignorance takes us down wrong paths is no guide at all. So how do we discern the marks of maturity that make for a trustworthy guide or friend? How do we find someone who will allow for the right emotional and spiritual fit? The next chapter will offer some tested pointers.

FOR FURTHER REFLECTION

• Read Luke 1:5-56. Note the ways in which Mary encouraged Elizabeth. Then note the ways Elizabeth helped Mary. If God was powerful enough to use an angel to communicate the plan to the two women, why did they still need each other?

• List below some of the ways in which you think a spiritual friend or guide could help you. What, for example, are some of your greatest needs in your relationship to God? Can you think of times you have said to yourself (or another), "I wish I had someone to talk to about my spiritual struggles"?

_____

_____

• Recall a relationship in your past where your expectations exceeded the reality. Think of ways your disappointment or hurt might tempt you to guard yourself and keep your needs and feelings to yourself.

• In the space provided below, list any hesitations or objections that make you wary of turning to a friend or spiritual guide. Compare these to your list above of ways a spiritual companion could help. Which list seems more compelling?

_____

_____

_____

TWO WOMEN'S GIFT OF FRIENDSHIP

When we hear the New Testament story of Mary and Elizabeth, it is easy to be struck by the miraculous fanfare surrounding the birth of their sons. Amid the angelic announcements, we may miss Luke's moving portrait of the two women's friendship and the way God used it to encourage them in faithfulness.

While they were cousins, their special friendship as we know it had beginnings in Luke 1, where we read of Gabriel's appearance to Elizabeth's husband. Even though they "both were getting on in years" (v. 7), Gabriel tells Zechariah that their son John (later known as John *the Baptist*) would be "great in the sight of the Lord" (v. 15).

Soon Mary herself receives a visit from Gabriel, this one even more rattling than Elizabeth's. While Elizabeth conceived in her old age, Mary learns that she would conceive Jesus in her virginity by the Holy Spirit (v. 35).

I believe it no accident in Luke's storytelling that almost immediately Mary left to find Elizabeth. She needed the encouragement and counsel this older, spiritually mature woman could give. "Mary set out and went with haste to a Judean town in the hill country, where she entered the house of Zechariah and greeted Elizabeth" (vv. 39-40).

"Mary's was the more costly miracle," a friend of mine once observed. "She had lost her reputation; her life would never be the same. No one understood. Except Elizabeth. What the Holy Spirit had brought to life in her leaped in recognition of what the same Spirit had conceived in Mary. And she was to say exactly what Mary needed to hear: 'Blessed are you' " (v. 42).

The story does not end with Elizabeth's blessing. Mary bursts into the exultant praises known as the *Magnificat* (Latin for the first word of Mary's song in vv. 46-55). Her outbreak of prophecy and thanksgiving to God must have been a reassuring gift to Elizabeth. No wonder the two women stayed together, as Luke tells us, for "about three months" (v. 56). ﾑﾐ

THREE

The Unshakable Companion

Here we are, you and I, and I hope a third, Christ, is in our midst.
                                                    Aelred of Rievaulx

Friendship is a sheltering tree.
                                        Samuel Taylor Coleridge

*Some friends play at friendship
but a true friend sticks closer than one's nearest kin.*
                                                    Proverbs 18:24

❧

ome years ago, an unexpected letter and package of books arrived in the mail from Jim, a friend I had just met at a church conference.

Jim was a struggling author with a balding head, flourishing beard, and warm eyes. It was in response to a conversation we had during a break at the conference that he mailed the books. Because my wife and I were pioneering a new church project in a suburb of Houston, the three volumes were a special gift: Each provided an account of some Christian's radical attempt to live out of trust in God for daily needs. The most striking was the biography of nineteenth-century English church leader George Müller.[1] Each volume, Jim told me in his letter, had helped convince him "that it is possible to live by faith," to place even daily matters "in God's hands." In letters to come, he wrote about his own setbacks and successes as he experimented with trusting God for his everyday needs. The books and his experiences made me more aware of God's ability to provide.

When my family and I felt called a couple years later to make an important—but risky—move from Houston to a small Indiana town hundreds of miles away, we no longer insisted, as we once might have, on settling every detail related to our future income. Jim had opened our eyes to God's ability to provide and helped us brave uncertainty to make one of the most significant moves we have ever made as a family. My friend's simplicity and faith had become contagious.

Our most significant encounters with others often are unspectacular. And usually they involve rather ordinary people. It is tempting to look for help from the spiritual "experts," to those whose every other sentence is a quotation from scripture, who seem to exude a heroic holiness. But the qualities that make for life-changing companionship are surprisingly simple and probably resident in a number of people you already know.

What are they? How do we recognize someone who can helpfully walk beside us? Or, you may wonder, how do we avoid opening our lives to someone who lacks the maturity to understand us? Or who might love nothing better than to adopt us as a "mission project"? There are several traits or qualities to look for in a spiritual guide. Here are five of the most important.

THE OPENNESS OF A LISTENING FRIEND

We first need someone who will encourage our honest sharing and growth in insight by listening. When it comes to dryness in our prayer life, for example, we may tend to think only in terms of hard advice or "practical" solutions.

But great healing and insight can come simply by spending time in the presence of someone who hears us out.

The martyred German Christian pastor Dietrich Bonhoeffer speaks of listening as nothing less than a *ministry*. "Many people," he writes, "are looking for an ear that will listen. They do not find it among Christians, because these Christians are talking where they should be listening. . . . One who cannot listen long and patiently will presently be talking beside the point and be never really speaking to others."[2] Having someone greet our sharing or questioning with chatter quickly confirms that mere lecturing will do little to help. To help, our friend or mentor must usually resist the temptation to jump in with a premature solution. He or she will not settle for merely "fixing" our immediate problem but will let the whole picture emerge.

We first need someone who will encourage our honest sharing and growth in insight by listening . . . . Great healing and insight can come simply by spending time in the presence of someone who hears us out.

If we struggle with lust or sexual temptation, for example, we need more than to be handed a list of scripture verses on purity. We need someone who will help us sort through the larger issues, such as a need for approval, or unmet emotional needs in marriage, or simple lack of mental discipline. A friend or mentor needs to listen first, not just fire off a prescription for the presenting problem. Deeper insights—and true solutions—usually take time to emerge.

A woman I know was struggling to make sense of a particularly troubling time in her life. Two miscarriages left her doubting God's care. Further, she reasoned to her spiritual friend, God knows everything anyway, so why bother to pray? "In a loving way," she recalls, "my friend said he couldn't completely answer those questions. He heard me out. He didn't react with horror or condescension. *Then* he reminded me that sometimes prayer is simply a matter of obedience. So I decided I would pray simply to obey. I began to pray out of something deeper than feelings. I believe if I hadn't done that my prayer life would never have come back. But my friend listened before he spoke, and that made the difference."

My wife told me of a painful college experience that illustrates what can happen otherwise. Her classmates had told her about a freshman adviser who was well liked, so my wife went to her with high hopes. Taking her class schedule to be signed, she freely told the woman about some of her difficulties with college life. In the middle of Jill's talking, the adviser interrupted to correct Jill's grammar. She made it clear, without so many words, that she wasn't interested in hearing what a struggling young student had to say. My wife never shared deeply with her again.

Little things can tell us if someone will be a good listener—for example, eyes that stay fixed upon us as we talk, as though nothing could distract their attention. Or posture: I once heard someone describe a good listener by saying, "He *leans forward*—toward me—when I talk; it feels like he's willing to be intensely involved." A person who always conveys the impression of being in a hurry may disappoint us. All these signals can tip us off to whether someone may be willing to invest energy in listening, and thereby help us feel valued.

Listening is important for another reason. Someone who takes time to listen is much more likely to offer counsel or encouragement that truly fits. A good listener will accurately understand our need or situation. My friend Jim, for example, *heard* something while we talked at the conference that helped him know that certain books would help me.

Even if we are turning to a mentor—a wiser, more mature companion—we still need to expect space and quiet to be ourselves and talk about what is happening deep within. One characteristic of good spiritual direction is to "get out of the way," Eugene H. Peterson writes, "to be unimportant. A paradox is in operation here: to be *really* present without being *obtrusively* present."[3]

When we share some harebrained rationale for doing wrong, we need more than nodding silence. Effective companionship begins with a willingness to sit still long enough to listen and let insight emerge.

I have a friend who discovered this. The companion who taught her more about the spiritual life than any other, she remembers, was careful not to give quick advice. "We'd go out on a bike ride," she explains, "and she'd let me talk while she just listened. She generally didn't give an opinion, at least not right off. She'd ask me probing questions that would bring me to my next step."

This is not to say that listening alone is enough. When we share some harebrained rationale for doing wrong, we need more than nodding silence. Effective companionship begins with a willingness to sit still long enough to listen and let insight emerge. Growth in Christ is more than a matter of accumulating information. It is listening for the will of the Father, staying alert to what the turns in our lives are telling us, and approaching God—along with someone else—with an open ear.

Listening like this means that a spiritual companion will not just sit quietly passive. Listening has an active side. A friend will know when not to be quick with words but also when to probe. Simple, direct questions can sometimes draw out themes or issues we may gloss over. Questions may shed more light on our situation than hours of lectures. Indeed, the artful use of questions has a history of proven value in the Christian life, dating back to Jesus himself. "Jesus," writes seminary professor Margaret Guenther, "had a way of sweeping distractions out of the way with a trenchant question. To the blind beggar Bartimaeus he asked: 'What do you want me to do for you?' To the disciples of John the Baptist, as they crept along behind him, attracted yet cautious: 'What do you seek?' To the disciples, despairing of having enough to feed the multitude: 'How many loaves have you? Go and see.' The four gospels alone provide enough questions for spiritual directors [or spiritual friends] to use in clearing away the clutter and helping the directee articulate a yearning for God."[4]

THE ENCOURAGEMENT OF A CARING FRIEND

Second, a spiritual friend or mentor should create an encouraging climate. Just as important as being listened to is feeling accepted and understood. A companion who tells us, "I'm here, I'll stay—even if you do not have all of your life put together" frees us to grow. Such a friend helps us not grow weary and lose the hope that keeps us trying. Some of the most powerful changes within us will be spurred on by affirmation, not criticism; by support, not faultfinding.

My friend and prayer partner Kevin once articulated how important this quality of encouragement was to him. "When we first started meeting," he said, "almost every week I had to admit that I had given practically no time to prayer the week before. As that went on week after week, it became harder for me to see myself as a spiritual giant. I had to admit that for all my talk, sometimes I don't care about prayer or reading the scriptures.

"But every week, I found that you would listen to me. I realized, 'You're going to like me even if I'm like this.' It was freeing to understand I could just be who I was. It actually motivated me to pray more."

A companion who tells us, "I'm here, I'll stay——even if you do not have all of your life put together" frees us to grow. Such a friend helps us not grow weary and lose the hope that keeps us trying.

I remember a time I faced a painful situation with little of that kind of encouragement. A couple of members of a church I served as pastor, once ardent supporters, became vocally critical of my leadership. They shared their criticisms with other church members. Conflict began to snowball. I needed a soul friend, but my wife and I faced the pain largely alone. I vowed never to have to go through such discouragement without a supportive friend with whom I could freely share.

The wife of a pastor whose church had just erupted in conflict once told a small support group I was leading, "Sometimes I just want to express my tangled feelings and know I will be heard, know I am still OK." She wanted us to remember that our support was the one essential ingredient in her time of great need. Encouragement does not equal unquestioning acceptance, of course. Sometimes a friend will see through our second-best, halfhearted efforts and point to the better good he or she sees latent in us. The New Testament word sometimes translated *encourage* means more than just saying nice things; it also suggests calling out something deeper or truer from another. "As you know, we dealt with each one of you like a father with his children," Paul wrote the church at Thessalonica, "urging and encouraging you and pleading that you lead a life worthy of God" (1 Thess. 2:11-12). But the overall atmosphere clearly bespeaks love.

I remember years ago working with a colleague on an important writing assignment. My partner was not shouldering her responsibilities, to the point that our project, in which I had invested a great deal of energy, was imperiled. As I talked it all through with Kevin, he did more than nod in understanding of my frustration. He prayed with me, supported me in my legitimate frustration, and helped me know that I was not alone when it came time to insist that my colleague deliver. I gained strength from the presence of another.

The great Christian leader Basil eloquently wrote centuries ago that the spiritual guide, "must care for weak souls with tenderness and humility of heart . . . . He [or she] must be compassionate and long-suffering with those who through inexperience fall short in duty. He [or she] should not pass over their sins in silence, but must bear gently with the sinner, applying remedies in all kindness and moderation." It was with that sentiment in mind that spiritual writer Richard J. Foster once described a good spiritual companion as one who is "unjudging and unshakable."[5] We need to find a friend who will be slow to judge and whose presence and insight will encourage us to be the best we can be.

THE TOUGHNESS OF AN HONEST FRIEND

As pleasant as it is to be supported, sometimes we need to hear a caution or receive a correction. This is particularly true when we feel ourselves in a rut or are too close to a situation to see clearly. We all need at least one person who will help us stay honest with others—and ourselves.

I once talked to a man whose church put interested men together for accountability. This is how he described it to me: "A friend of mine and I meet each Friday. We sit down one-on-one, and we go through questions about commitment from a book on Christian men. We have come to see a lot of things that we didn't want to admit about ourselves. My partner will call me to see my blind spots, whereas before I did not want to admit them or do anything about them." While his partner was not out to criticize, he had the courage to ask the probing, potentially uncomfortable question.

I know of a pastor who meets with a group of colleagues who challenge each other with several questions periodically. They include: Have any of your financial dealings lacked integrity? Have you exposed yourself to any sexually explicit material? Have you spent adequate time in Bible study and prayer? Have you given priority time to your family? and, Have you just lied to me? An inventory like this can be valuable to more than just pastors.

It takes a commitment to growth to face issues such as these. And sometimes it takes a surprising amount of courage to confront another person we care about. Anyone we approach for spiritual friendship or mentoring must be strong enough in his or her self-image to risk our irritation when we react to a confrontive word. Confronting another is something I have had to learn to do; it does not come naturally, and a part of me still fears being rejected when I share criticism with another. But a friend or mentor should be able and willing to say the hard word that we may greet coolly or defensively at first.

One time I talked with Kevin about my wife. I don't recall what I said, but Kevin sensed in what I shared that I was not valuing her enough. Kevin reminded me of the ministry she was having by homeschooling our boys, by temporarily giving up career goals while the children were small. Kevin rightly brought a word of correction.

But the story did not end there. Shortly after the conversation, Kevin later recounted to me,

> I started considering going back to graduate school full time. I wanted my wife to work full time to support our family, even though she felt uncomfortable with that idea. As I shared this with you, you said, How does this fit with what you were telling me recently about *my wife* and her ministry in the family? I realized I was being selfish, thinking only about my own educational ambitions and not about what was best for our entire family.

THE RESPECT OF A HUMBLE FRIEND

Even if we ask someone to be a mentor, a person who in some ways we perceive as more than a mere peer, whomever we meet with must not look down on us. For the challenges of another not to provoke us to discouragement, the person we seek out must be capable of relating to us out of respect.

Some years ago I shared with a spiritual mentor my frustration with a car (our family's only one at the time) that was on its last tires. The issue as I shared it had to do with learning not to "worry about anything" as Paul says in Philippians 4:6. Her well-intentioned response was to suggest how to find an inexpensive replacement for our ailing vehicle or supplement my income with a part-time job. She was ready with advice, but I felt she was subtly conveying that I could not capably mind the practicalities of life. Even if I was overspiritualizing my dilemma, her practical prescriptions (all of which I had thought of) failed to take seriously the larger issues involved and reduced the conversation to her brainstorming "how-tos." She rushed to "mend" me before she had completely listened or appreciated my dilemma.

I like the way a friend of mine described the way her spiritual mentor, an older, wiser woman, helped her feel this respect: "She did not get me 'hooked' on her in a dependent relationship. I felt from her a deep respect and the belief that I can hear for myself what God might be saying or how God might be leading. She encouraged me time and time again to listen to what I was hearing and be confident of that voice." Her spiritual life grew immeasurably from the presence of this spiritually gifted friend, who made space for her friend and pointed away from herself.

THE WISDOM OF A SPIRIT-MINDED FRIEND

The primary quality needed in a helper is devotion to Christ and sensitivity to God. The center of spiritual friendship has to do with our relationship with him, with becoming more like Christ, with letting the Spirit rule in every area of life. The person we turn to must therefore have a certain amount of wisdom or maturity. He or she need not be a spiritual genius but should be someone who prays, who sees spiritual growth as a priority, and who can bring spiritual sensitivity to the relationship. We need to watch for people whose spiritual commitment we respect and admire and wish to emulate.

A friend was telling me about someone who was a spiritual mentor for her. "I could see in him," she told me, "an intimate relationship with God." She was drawn to this quality, she said, because "I'd been praying in my own life that the Lord would give me an intimate relationship. As I spent time with my friend who prays a great deal, it dawned on me that intimacy comes through prayer, through simply spending time with God." What he modeled and what he said pointed my friend to the Father.

Paul the apostle captured the significance of this. He wrote, "We do not proclaim ourselves; we proclaim Jesus Christ as Lord and ourselves as your slaves for Jesus' sake" (2 Cor. 4:5). That is the focus of any effort to grow in spiritual maturity. This is why Paul prayed for one church under his charge, "I pray that the God of our Lord Jesus Christ, the Father of glory, may give you a spirit of wisdom and revelation as you come to know him" (Eph. 1:17). In Christian friendship we look not for mere personality or human ingenuity but for one who knows and understands God, who can share with us in the great adventure of faith.

FOR FURTHER REFLECTION

• Read 1 Samuel 18:1-9; 23:15-18; and 2 Samuel 1. In what ways was Jonathan and David's friendship indispensable in the working out of God's purposes for each man's life—and for the nation of Israel? In what ways did the qualities of a mentor and friend noted in this chapter come into play?

• Name the five people who have had the greatest positive impact on your life. Your list may contain the names, for example, of a parent, work colleague, or minister. Try to include people from both childhood and adulthood. Now, list the traits or qualities that made these people so important to your growth.

• Which of the five traits enumerated in this chapter are the most important to you? Is finding someone who will be kind and affirming more important to you than finding someone who can be tough? Do you agree that spiritual wisdom and maturity are among the most important qualities of a spiritual guide?

• Take a sheet of paper and write the qualities you would look for in an ideal spiritual helper. Make a list of the people you know who best demonstrate the traits mentioned in this chapter and in your paragraph(s). Can you envision any of them being your spiritual friend? If so, begin thinking about how you might approach them.

THE DIFFERENCE A HUSBAND AND WIFE MADE

The New Testament story of Priscilla and Aquila makes a compelling case for one-on-one (in their case, two-on-one) Christian nurture. It is fair to say that the course of early church history was changed because of their faithful relationship building.

The nurturing impulse of this husband-and-wife team, Acts tells us, found expression one day when a traveling teacher named Apollos came to Ephesus (Acts 18:24). While he was an "eloquent man, well-versed in the scriptures," his education was not complete. He knew "only the baptism of John" [the Baptist] (v. 25). While Apollos spoke "boldly" and "with burning enthusiasm," he didn't know the whole story.

Here is where Priscilla and Aquila came in. As soon as they heard him speak they "took him aside and explained the Way of God to him more accurately" (v. 26). It wasn't that the couple didn't have better things to do; Paul listed them as persons who "work with me," noting that they once even risked their lives for him (Rom. 16:3-4). They also had a church that met regularly in their house (1 Cor. 16:19). The pair nevertheless invested themselves personally in Apollos, pulling him aside for individual counsel and instruction.

That Paul could later chide some of the Corinthian Christians for divisions, some siding with Paul and others with Apollos, suggests the impact Apollos came to have in the early church. He no doubt owed at least some of his influential ministry to the day an alert couple invited him over for teaching—with a personal touch. ༚

FOUR

The Options of Friendship

Just as there is no universal remedy which is prescribed for every disease, so also there is no general guidance so perfect that every person, with his [or her] particular needs, can be helped by it.
Francis Quilloré, Seventeenth-Century French Christian

There is no problem, it seems to me, in collecting from many different flowers the honey which we cannot find in one flower only.
Francis de Sales

ᕫ

friend once told me of a time when he struggled with a constant, seemingly unconquerable compulsion. "I was sincere in wanting to quit, but I seemed unable to stop." In his frustration, he turned to two men who were to help him in very different but complementary ways. Charles went first to his counseling instructor at college, who was also a hospital chaplain. "He had little advice," Charles told me, "but communicated what I can only call unconditional acceptance. I find it hard to say what he did for me in that encounter, except to say that he conveyed an acceptance I had never before experienced. It has kept me going ever since."

But Charles did not stop there. He went to a philosophy instructor who, Charles recalls, "took me to the great fourth-century leader Augustine," a writer and thinker who talked about the importance of using your will in the Christian life.

While this second friend was accepting and caring, he also urged Charles to believe that change was possible, that Christian faith brings power to resolve struggles and end undesirable actions.

Charles discovered that each man contributed something different but vital. Through one, he learned to accept himself and trust God's ability to love him, whatever his failings. Through the other, he was nudged and pushed to believe that he must and, just as important, *could* change.

Spiritual friendship, as Charles's experience illustrates, is a many-splendored thing. We should be wary of assuming there is only one way to find it. The people we turn to may come from a range of age groups. They may be more advanced than we in Christian maturity, or they may be spiritual peers. And we may find that looking to one person for all our needs for spiritual support may not be realistic. We need to be flexible and creative.

MENTOR OR FRIEND?

Should we look for someone who seems farther along spiritually or a friend more or less at the same place? Both have ample precedent in the Bible (in, for example, the peer relationship of Jonathan and David, or the spiritual father/spiritual son relationship of Paul and Timothy). Both have advantages.

With a mutual mentor or friend, you help each other and in turn are helped. The arrangement has the benefit of constantly sending the message that we can help another person, even when we have questions, problems, or areas needing prayer. If we are always going to someone with needs, we may soon feel we have little to offer others. Self-esteem may suffer.

"The nice thing about mutual mentoring," my friend Kevin observes, "is that every time you admit you have struggles, you are also able in that same meeting to give to somebody else and help him or her. I think that's healthy." Also, if our partners always have to have all the answers, they may fall into the trap of seeing themselves as spiritual virtuosos.

Furthermore, a mutual mentor, by virtue of his or her sharing our stage of spiritual development, may be asking the same questions we are and thus be uniquely able to relate to our issues. I know of two men who call their helping relationship *co-mentoring*. They are roughly the same age. Both have families, and they share a profession. And they both, as one of them puts it, "have a love for the Bible that's rubbed off on one another." But for all their similarities, they still bring different strengths. One accents Christian character as the mark of spiritual maturity. He is likely to ask his partner, "Are you loving your wife?" The other emphasizes prayer and devotional disciplines and would tend to ask his partner, "How faithful have you been in your time with God?" Their mutual mentoring allows for a spiritual cross-fertilization even though neither is markedly more mature.

On the other hand, you may want to consider turning to a mentor who is clearly older and wiser. You may want tested wisdom and the benefit of another's years of growing and learning. This holds especially true for those new in the faith or those exploring new areas of faithfulness or fruitfulness. Writer Tilden Edwards even believes that it is usually best to choose a partner in his or her second half of life: roughly thirty-five or older. "Before this age," he reasons, "illusions of infinitude, ambition for a niche in the human community, and trust in salvation by techniques (everything will be fine with just a little more education, therapy, money, intimacy, etc.) tend to lurk behind attitudes and behaviors."[1] I would not go as far as Tilden Edwards; sometimes the zeal of someone younger may counterbalance any limitations of a relatively young perspective. But there is often a place for the tested experience of an older friend or mentor.

My friend Carol discovered this. When she was still a young Christian in her twenties, she sat in church one Sunday while a couple who worked with mentally and physically challenged children talked about their work and asked for prayer. "I felt strongly this is what I should do even though I had never done it before and was a bit afraid of people with disabilities." It worked out so that Carol spent the next year living in the couple's household. Through being with them, watching how they treated the children in their care, learning how God used them to love, she recalls, "I learned to serve people as Christ would serve." She learned some valuable lessons only a couple more experienced in the Christian life could give.

I once heard someone reflect that at the church he used to attend, "The age ranges in the Sunday school classes were all over the place. There was so much interaction of different ages. At the church I go to now, Sunday school members tend to be segregated by age. We're all experiencing a lot of the same stuff in life, and yet I think the younger ones are missing out on some wisdom." If church or work doesn't offer many opportunities to interact with elders, a mentor may provide some richness and perspective we might not find otherwise.

In considering a mentor, remember ways in which age—and age differences—may color your spiritual friendship. Psychologist Daniel Levinson suggests that at least among men, a person will tend to see other persons as peers if they are not more than six or seven years older or younger. When someone is eight to fifteen years older, a man will quite naturally regard him or her as we would an older brother or sister. A man of forty is regarded by people in their twenties as "Dad" rather than a buddy. In an age difference of forty years, the elder will assume the symbolic properties of a grandparent.[2]

Which is better for you: an older mentor or a mutual friend? Each kind of partner has potential value. The important thing is to be aware of the options and to prayerfully clarify what it is we most need. Throughout this book I principally focus on spiritual friendship. But most of what I suggest applies to mentoring relationships. And I will occasionally refer specifically to spiritual direction, which implies a difference between the two people.

And consider this: If you find yourself drawn to people in one age category only, you may want to expand your horizons. You may want the blessings of relating to a contemporary rounded out by the lessons to be gained from a spiritual senior.

HIM AND HER?

People often wonder if men and women can relate together successfully in a mentoring relationship or friendship. One woman, calling in during a radio talk show I participated in, put it like this: "I'm single due to divorce, and I prayed for someone of the opposite sex who would help me see things from the man's perspective because I didn't have that kind of relationship. And the Lord provided someone like that for me. Do you think it can work?"

I gave a qualified yes. Men and women can offer one another mutually enriching and complementary insights. Christian history provides several examples of this: Francis of Assisi and Clare, Teresa of Avila and John of the Cross, Evelyn Underhill and Baron Friedrich von Hügel. But the greater risks must be acknowledged. Attraction between the two sexes can be deceptively powerful. And my caller would be wiser to find the "man's perspective" from a small group that included men and women.

I do know a few people who believe it can work. A friend I'll call Susan found her pastor to be a true spiritual mentor. "There are a lot of reasons to favor female-female or male-male relationships," she admits. "But John was more effective for me because he was not only a true person of prayer but an authority figure, and a lot of the healing I've needed in my personal and spiritual life concerns male authority figures." In this case, I would add, the presence of a defined role helped keep the relationship focused on spiritual priorities.

Another reason it worked has to do with the safeguards Susan and John talked about and built in when they began meeting for spiritual conversation and prayer.

If they met at the church office, it was only when the secretary or someone else could be there. Susan also shared with her husband all that she and her pastor discussed. "We realized that one reason we could do it was that we each had strong marriages. We weren't going to look to the other for what we found in our spouses. And we agreed that we would not talk about our spouses or our marriages. That could set up an inappropriate intimacy." Safeguards such as these will help spiritual friends avoid even the appearance of evil.

I also believe that a healthy difference in ages can help. The dynamics of attraction may lessen, though not disappear, when a thirty-year-old man seeks counsel from a fifty-year-old woman.

"Many persons," writes pastor Barry Woodbridge in his *A Guidebook for Spiritual Friends*, "can have a spiritual friend of the opposite sex if they are clear about their motivations for seeking that person. As a rule, though, you may find it simpler and clearer if this is not the case."[3] Seeking spiritual help from a person of the opposite sex can remain an option, then. But it does require that both persons go in with eyes wide open and appropriate safeguards in place.

WHERE TWO OR THREE ARE GATHERED

While most of this book assumes a one-on-one relationship, sometimes mentoring can happen effectively by involving more than one. When two people are inexperienced in giving spiritual guidance, the safeguards of a threesome's collective wisdom may be indispensable. A married couple may also be ideal friends or mentors for either an individual or couple. When my wife and I were engaged, we met weekly with another engaged Christian couple to talk about the emotional and spiritual issues involved in preparing for marriage. We were uniquely able to help one another sort through the issues we all faced.

Several years ago, I would meet with two other men from my church for an hour and a half every other

Saturday. Because we all had young children and wanted to guard our weekend family times, we started at seven A.M. As we met, we talked about what God wanted us to be as husbands, fathers, church members, and employees. We shared questions about our progress in faithfulness and scripture verses that had helped us in the time since our last meeting. One of us would read a passage from the Bible, and then we would go around the circle and talk about our lives. We ended with informal, spontaneous prayer for one another.

"It had been quite a while since I could share deeply with other men," Steve remembers of the group. "But it meant so much to have a close enough relationship to let down the masks and be known at a deep level."

When two people are inexperienced in giving spiritual guidance, the safeguards of a threesome's collective wisdom may be indispensable.

An ambitious group approach worked well for another friend. She joined three women who agreed to meet regularly for one year for the express purpose of encouraging spiritual growth. Each was to write in her journal regularly, read scripture, pray, read an assigned book on some aspect of the spiritual life, and bring to each weekly meeting the discoveries and struggles of the week. The women all came out of the year deeper in their faith and stronger in their commitment.

It is interesting that John Wesley, the founder of Methodism, also relied on a kind of group-centered spiritual mentoring. He was struggling to help new converts grow in their spiritual maturity. The solution came in a surprising way.

When the Methodists contracted a debt to build a "preaching house," leaders volunteered to visit each member weekly to collect a penny. But they soon found it was easier for the people to come to each leader. As people gathered for these "class meetings," the focus changed. Class leaders began to use the times to keep track of members' spiritual lives. Members opened up and talked about their progress and setbacks in living the Christian life; the group discussed the issues raised; and the meeting was closed with specific prayer for each person there.

HELP FROM MANY SOURCES

Even if we opt for a one-on-one approach, we may find it helpful not to rely on just one such relationship; there is no need to limit ourselves to one companion or guide. You may have several different areas of your life for which you long for conversation. One person may not be able to do that. You may want to find a different partner for different areas of growth.

After years of meeting with Kevin to focus on spiritual growth, for example, I sensed God nudging me to grow in my leadership abilities. I approached an older, widely experienced leader in the church and asked if we could meet together every month or so to talk about what it means to be a leader. I soon found his astute questions and kindly encouragement deepening my understanding of ways God wanted to use me. He had a way of asking questions about my personal goals I had not even thought of. Our meetings encouraged me to grow intentionally in a specialized area.

The people who walk in and out of our lives can make a world of difference. We need only think of the possibilities awaiting our creativity and initiative.

FOR FURTHER REFLECTION

• Compare the relationships of Paul and Timothy (2 Tim. 1:1-6) and Jonathan and David (1 Sam. 18:1-9; 23:15-18). How were they different? How did God use these two very different partnerships to accomplish God's ends?

• Think about friends to whom you relate as peers. Do their ages confirm Levinson's assertion that peers are not more than six or seven years older or younger?

• Make a list of acquaintances who, while they may not be professionally trained, are people in whom you could confide your spiritual questions.

• Take a sheet of paper. On the top of the left half write *peers*. On the top of the right half write *elders*. Now list the advantages of each under the headings. Which seems better suited to your needs?

• What question or questions do you have about relating to God? Ask your question of more than one person. Does your experience confirm Charles's, that different people can offer a different, but complementary, perspective? What implications does this have for finding one or more spiritual companions?

THE NIGHT GOD CALLED SAMUEL

The story of the prophet Samuel's call provides a fascinating case study in spiritual mentoring—mentoring that becomes mutual in a surprising way.

The story is set in the temple of ancient Israel. The boy Samuel served as assistant to the temple priest Eli, we learn in 1 Samuel 3. Then verse 4 tells us simply, "Then the Lord called, 'Samuel!'" The boy heard God calling his name.

But Samuel did not understand. Samuel "did not yet know the Lord," verse 7 explains. Night though it was, the boy twice ran to Eli and said, "Here I am." Eli twice told Samuel to go back to bed. Even Eli, for all his age and wisdom, did not understand. But the third time we read, "Eli perceived that the Lord was calling the boy. Therefore Eli said to Samuel, 'Go, lie down; and if he calls you, you shall say, "Speak, Lord, for your servant is listening".'" (vv. 8-9)

This time, thanks to the discernment and wise counsel of his mentor, Samuel waited on God, and God again spoke. The young prophet's career was launched. In an intriguing twist, the Lord's first word to Samuel is a message for Eli. The one who helped Samuel listen stands in need of a message himself. The Lord is about to carry out judgment against Eli and his rebellious sons. "The Lord said to Samuel: 'See, I am about to do something in Israel that will make both ears of anyone who hears of it tingle. On that day I will fulfill against Eli all that I have spoken concerning his house' " (vv. 11-12). It was a hard word, but through it God reminded the people of Israel that God was still in charge, still speaking, and God would use whatever it took—even an old man and a young boy—to accomplish God's work among the people. ⸿

FIVE

Taking the Plunge

Test the physician before you open yourself to him. Determine whether he can be ill with one who is ill, weep with one who weeps. See whether he imparts instruction with gentleness and forbearance.

Origen, Third-Century Christian Philosopher

Join in imitating me, and observe those who live according to the example you have in us.

Philippians 3:17

❧

For my friend Beth, the decision to ask Sherry to be a spiritual friend was a year coming. After months of bumping into her at church or hearing her pray in a small prayer group, Beth finally mustered the courage. Beth realized that her life would be richer, her commitment more rooted, if she became intentional about time spent with Sherry. It wasn't just that Sherry was some thirty years older. "She had spiritual wisdom," Beth recalled. "I realized she was the kind of woman I wanted to become." Sherry, for her part, seemed to express a special interest in Beth, giving a call or dropping a note after times she prayed with Beth at church or prayer meetings.

But it took a while to become a reality. Why the delay?

"I was busy," Beth recalls. "Sherry was busy, and I wasn't sure how she would respond to my asking her to be my friend and mentor." But when Beth hit a time of spiritual dryness and depression, she realized it was time. "One Sunday Sherry came up and asked me how I was. I finally just blurted it out: 'I need a spiritual friend and mentor. Would you consider being that for me?'"

As they began meeting, Beth discovered that her new-found prayer partner and friend had herself gone through a time of depression years before. "It made me realize," Beth explains, "that this was the person God had for me. God guided me to her."

For all the benefits of having a friend or mentor like Beth found, many Christians have never taken the step. We recognize the value of finding such a helper, but we hesitate. What holds us back? Several practical barriers may confront us.

Schedules may be a factor. "I work late a number of nights in the week," someone once objected to me, "and I have a family; the prospect of taking on another relationship makes me think, *I have trouble fitting in the ones with my children and wife as it is, to say nothing of my ongoing church commitments!*"

My friend Karen has another view, however. She started meeting weekly with a prayer partner, despite working on a master's degree program, tending to the needs of a husband and two children, and being active in her church. "I'm really busy, but I live for that hour every week," she told me.

David Mains and Steve Bell are right in stressing that a prayer partner "could be the *answer* to your troubles, not just one more item screaming for attention."[1] The wisdom of a friend in the Spirit, far from burdening us more, may actually help us get our schedules under control—and under the eye of Christ. Besides, a thriving spiritual life has a way of increasing our energy and effectiveness. Our lives come to resemble more fully the trees of Psalm 1, "planted by streams of water, which yield their fruit in its season, and their leaves do not wither" (v. 3). Grounding our lives in the nourishment of friendship and the safeguards of accountability is more likely to replenish our reserves than drain them.

Another practical barrier may have to do with reservations that our request may be "imposing" on another. We are reluctant to face the awkward response of someone who feels he or she simply cannot "take us on." This was an issue for Beth as she thought about asking Sherry to mentor her. "But I realized that we all have gifts," she recalls. "If someone—like Sherry—has a gift, she probably *wants* to use it. It encourages the person when we ask." Far more than we realize, people will be honored—and eager—to share with us in the grand adventure of spiritual growth. And if we ask someone who has to say no, we have to remember that is a response to overcommitment rather than to us.

Still another barrier: We fear we won't know how to spend a regular, designated time, that we may have trouble finding things to say. Whatever the initial awkwardness of sharing at the depths, people in spiritual partnerships I know never come up short on material for conversation and prayer. If we are opening our lives to God on an ongoing basis, if we are reading the scriptures with any kind of regularity, if we are striving at all to be faithful in the daily round of our ordinary life, much is happening that we can bring before another for prayerful reflection.

Scrutinizing obstacles like these usually makes them shrink. A friend of mine, learning of my interest in spiritual helpers, wistfully remarked, "I don't have someone in my life like that, but I wish I did." This socially competent spiritually committed man simply needs an encouraging nudge, along with suggestions for concrete steps to take to get spiritual friendship underway. What follows is a plan of action that can help.

START WITH PRAYER

The first and perhaps most important step is simple. *We pray.* If all the great writers on spiritual friendship and direction say anything in common, it is that true spiritual help is more than a human enterprise. God is the central actor in the partnership. Finding a spiritual partner must therefore also be a matter of seeking God's guidance. We need more than simple admiration or affinity for someone of like personality. Finding someone entails careful listening to more than our feelings but also to the guidance God might give.

My friend Kevin, when he was realizing the need for spiritual companionship before we met, started praying, "Lord, bring along the kind of person I need." Richard J. Foster tells of a similar first step: "I ask God to bring me someone and then I wait . . . . My first director was an older woman who worked nights in a large hospital . . . . [At] eight in the morning, the end of the night shift, we met together to learn about prayer and to share our experiences with God. We began to learn what it means to walk with Christ, and the experience was a wonderful one for both of us. But it began by asking God to give me someone who would travel the road with me."[2] It may be that God is simply waiting for our asking. Not all God's blessings come unsought or uninvited.

True spiritual help is more than a human enterprise. God is the central actor in the partnership.

We can bring an attitude of expectant trust to such praying. There is no reason to think that God cannot provide someone or help us find him or her. God has resources we cannot imagine and ways of communicating we don't know about. We need not worry about God's being miserly in giving us what we need to know. James says, "If any of you is lacking in wisdom, ask God, who gives to all generously and ungrudgingly, and it will be given you" (James 1:5).

God may be more eager to lead us to the right person than we think. For Beth it began, as she says, "with a vague thought about Sherry that kept increasing as I prayed and thought about it. When I got a warm letter from Sherry, I took that as confirmation."

This is not to say that we should expect God to save us from an occasional wrong turn or painful outcome. Even after we have prayed our options through, we never completely eliminate the need to take risks in our relationships. Praying can keep me open to God's sometimes surprising options, but it does not guarantee that I will always make perfect choices. Even so, we can trust that God will not leave us stranded as we search.

LOOK AMONG EVERYDAY PEOPLE

Once we have started praying, *we begin looking.* The first place to look for a spiritual friend is among the people we bump into daily—those who work in our offices, who cut our hair, share with us in civic responsibilities, attend our Sunday school class, or serve with us on church committees. These friends may have an experience to relate, a conviction to share, or encouragement to give. Prayerful attentiveness may help us learn things from them we might otherwise miss.

My friend Kathy went biking or walking frequently with her neighbor. As their friendship developed, they found themselves discussing more than their children's school achievements or the latest book they had read; they spoke of spiritual insights and struggles. Their relationship grew to the point they could pray for each other's doubts, joys, and areas for future growth. Because they were alert and because they focused their friendship on spiritual things, they found a depth they would never have had otherwise.

Sometimes friends, family members, pastors, or fellow church members may know potential helpers. Seminary teacher Ben Campbell Johnson found this out. As he began asking God to lead him to a spiritual director, he found that "one by one I rejected the names on my roster. Some were too [emotionally] close; others were colleagues on the same faculty, or persons about whom I felt some doubt. One person . . . was too busy; another, too far away . . . . None of the options seemed right for me." He seemed to draw a blank. "Assistance on this search came in a strange way," Johnson recalls. "A minister friend came for an appointment on a subject far removed from spiritual direction." During the conversation he mentioned someone and described him as a "deeply spiritual man." He even said, recalls Johnson, "I'd drive halfway across the country to spend a day with John." Johnson suddenly exclaimed to himself, "That's it! He's the man!" Johnson made an appointment, and he and his newfound helper soon had it settled that they would meet together as mutual mentors and friends.[3]

To prayer, then, we need to add watchfulness. And as we search, we should not overlook the obvious. Perhaps we could invite a grandparent, neighbor, or old friend into such a sharing at the depths. "God rides the lame horse and carves the rotten wood," Martin Luther once said, by which he meant that God uses ordinary, flawed people to accomplish God's purposes. The person who draws alongside me need not be perfect, just able to walk with me as I try to live more faithfully in the loving presence of God.

MIND THE NUTS AND BOLTS

At some point, we need to think how a companion might fit into the routines of life. When is the best time of day to meet? Should you meet several times a year, monthly, weekly? If the person you select is a two-hour drive away, think how the distance will affect the frequency of your meetings. Writer and seminary teacher Margaret Guenther tells about a special friend with whom meetings have to be infrequent:

She is English, a musician . . . as well as a sensitive lay theologian. She gives me something I cannot give myself. Except for her disapproval of my fondness for florid, late-nineteenth-century Russian piano music, she accepts and loves me as I am. I value her keen mind and uncompromising honesty; and although we have never analyzed it, I know that our friendship is equally valuable to her. Distance keeps us from meeting oftener than once a year, but each time there is a sense of homecoming and complete safety.[4]

Particularly if you anticipate getting together with your spiritual partner weekly, think about the potential impact on those closest to you. Communicate clearly with a spouse, child, or close friend what you are planning. Such openness may keep a spouse from resenting the time this new relationship takes. Or it may keep jealousy from taking root if someone close to you feels excluded or threatened. Most of the time, family members will willingly give us space and time to cultivate something as wholesome and beneficial as spiritual friendship.

One man I know decided to wait until he had been married several years before seeking out a spiritual companion. "My wife and I had a high-dependency relationship. We expected each other to be spouse, lover, confidant, and counselor. It would have been too threatening to her. But after being married five, six years, she knew she couldn't meet all my needs, and that was OK, that if I had a close friendship with another she wouldn't feel pushed aside or left out."

DON'T SHRINK BACK

Eventually, we need to settle on someone. Then we have to *ask someone* (assuming he or she hasn't asked us first).

What does the asking look (and sound) like? There is no "right" way. I generally find it helpful, however, to tell the person I approach that I want to grow in my Christian life, that I appreciate some quality about him or her, and that I think I (or we) could benefit from meeting together on a regular basis. At times I have even jotted notes to myself or rehearsed specifics of my request.

Perhaps this is the hardest step. It is one thing to believe that someone can befriend us in our deepest selves or mentor us in faith. It is another to risk the asking. Who knows? The person we ask may not understand our request and may think us odd. Or even worse, as one man who hesitated admitted, "I was afraid that I would be more interested in such a thing than my friend and that I would thereby place him in the awkward position of having to say no. I was worried that that would strain our existing friendship."

We may also fear that friends may think us too "spiritual." For all that churches talk about prayer, Christians sometimes have a peculiar awkwardness in talking about their relationships with God. And praying with another does move us to a level of intimacy that may take some getting used to.

Whenever I have decided to approach someone to be a spiritual friend or mentor, I usually take weeks before I actually ask. Part of it is '"sitting with" my initial decision, ensuring I'm making the best choice, and sometimes I end up deciding against someone as I think through things more clearly. But I find that the waiting is more often than not based in fear. My anxiety about actually *doing* it makes me ingenious in my excuses. I find plenty of reasons for postponing. For me, for all of us, the risks in asking are real.

This is especially true if we have leftover hurts from earlier painful relationships. In the wake of unheralded disappointment or betrayal, exposing ourselves again feels intimidating. We may have to pray through lingering fears that someone will reject us, that he or she might shrug off our longings as unimportant. Such an emotional block is usually not hastily overcome. We may need to turn to another and ask for prayer for emotional healing.

It may also help to keep in mind that finding a spiritual friend or mentor may take trial and error. We may encounter a no from the first person we ask. Or perhaps just as bad, a lukewarm yes. We may begin meeting with someone who eventually does not work out (chapter 7 offers help for that situation). It may not be easy. Scottish preacher Alexander Whyte once described the perseverance of the saints as falling down and getting up, falling down and getting up, falling down and getting up, all the way to heaven. That's not a bad note of realism for many of life's ventures, including cultivating the kind of friendship we are talking about here.

It is one thing to believe that someone can befriend us in our deepest selves or mentor us in faith. It is another to risk the asking.

I like to remember that big corporations are sometimes wary of hiring executives unless they have at least one failure on their professional record. Those who do not, they reason, have never risked enough to fail, have never had the wholesomely painful experience of learning from a mistake. We may learn, then, from our stumbling attempts at reaching out.

Whatever our hesitations, the loneliness and painful isolation of *not* having a friend in the Spirit may propel us to the point of holy desperation. It may bring us to a place where we are willing to risk looking foolish, vulnerable, or unsophisticated. Pastor and writer Bruce Larson once asked the Swiss Christian psychologist Paul Tournier, "How do you help your patients get rid of their fears?"

"I don't," he said. "Fear is wonderful. Everything that's

worthwhile in life is scary. Choosing a school, choosing a career, getting married, having kids—the good things are scary. Don't get rid of your fears; look for fear. Do the thing you're afraid to do."

If you're not sure about finding a spiritual helper, you may want to begin the process of seeking anyway. Your steps, even if faltering, will start you out on the journey. The benefits of opening our lives to another are well worth the risks.

FOR FURTHER REFLECTION

• Read the story of Samuel's call in 1 Samuel 3. What might have happened if Samuel never heard—or heeded—the advice of his elder Eli?

• Begin praying, if you have not already, for God to provide the right person to help in your spiritual journey. Perhaps say, "Lord, lead me to the person who can help me grow in my relationship to you. And give me patience while I wait for you to show me your will."

• Pray specifically about names that may come to your awareness in the next several days. If no one comes to mind, consider the possibility that while God might have someone in mind, the timing is not right. You might also turn to friends or pastors for advice on who can help. Combine your prayerful weighing with hardheaded thinking about how each possible helper might work. Narrow the possibilities.

• Find out what you can about the people you are considering from people who know them.

• By talking it over with a spouse or loved one, think clearly about the time involved in meeting regularly with a spiritual helper. How often will you meet? How far will you travel to get together? What other practical considerations need attention?

• Unless you feel strong reservations or have found no satisfactory name, take the plunge! Take the initiative and invite your prospect to be your helper and friend.

PORTRAIT OF TWO WOMEN

The Book of Ruth paints a poignant portrait of two women brought together by tragic circumstances. Ruth's unswerving devotion to Naomi and Naomi's mentoring, motherly care for Ruth forms the basis for one of the Hebrew scriptures' most-loved stories of family commitment.

In one sense, it is remarkable that the woman Ruth appears in Hebrew scriptures at all. She was a Moabite—a foreigner—who married one of Naomi's Israelite sons. Such intermarriage was frowned on by the Israelites.

When Naomi and Ruth became widows, they found themselves in desperate need. When Naomi decided to return to her homeland of Bethlehem, Ruth overcame her mother-in-law's protests and argued, "Do not press me to leave you or to turn back from following you! Where you go, I will go; Where you lodge, I will lodge" (Ruth 1:16).

Ruth and Naomi arrive just as the barley harvest is beginning. Ruth goes to the fields to glean food for them both. When Ruth meets Boaz, the fields' owner, Naomi intervenes. She gives wise advice to her daughter-in-law. She tells her how to win Boaz's attention (Ruth 3), which successfully ends in marriage, and ultimately a secure future for both women.

But that is not the end of the story. God used Naomi's mentoring of her daughter-in-law for larger purposes. Through it God chose Ruth for a higher calling than either could have imagined. When Ruth marries Boaz, she conceives and gives birth to Obed, the grandfather of David. The ultimate end of this genealogy, as Matthew 1:1-6 later tells us, is Jesus, the Messiah, and the greatest "son of David" of all. ᕫᕍ

SIX

Getting the Most Out of Spiritual Guidance

*We do not wish for friends to feed and clothe our bodies
. . . but to do the like office to our spirits.*
Henry David Thoreau

*We do not want you to become lazy, but to imitate those
who through faith and patience inherit what has been promised.*
Hebrews 6:12, NIV

᷇ᴥ

I need some suggestions," someone recently told me.
"I'm about to start meeting with a spiritual mentor,
and neither of us has ever done this before. What pointers
can you give?"

My friend realized meeting with a a spiritual companion
held great promise. She wanted to do more than stumble
into it. And she knew that what she and her partner brought
to the meetings could spell the difference between mere
pleasant conversation and life-changing growth.

How can we make the most of our friendship or mentoring relationship? What qualities should we cultivate?
What steps should we take?

SET UP GROUND RULES

Clarifying expectations is one of the first things to tend to. What can we rightfully expect—and not expect? My friend Karen underscores this: "When you start developing this kind of relationship, you're taking a risk. You're taking a step of intimacy. The clearer the expectations and guidelines, the better. Because if the expectations are not spoken, you form them anyway. And then you set yourself up for hurt."

Kevin once told me a story that illustrates this. When he was a freshman in college, living hours from home, struggling through a Midwest winter of record-breaking cold, he made a special friend in Mike, an older and wiser classmate.

The time they spent talking—in the hallways after class or in small group meetings in Mike's off-campus apartment—strengthened Kevin's faith. Mike became a guide and true friend.

But once Kevin had to face an unexpected temptation—on his own. When it was over, he was disappointed with himself and confused about the trustworthiness of his friend. He went to Mike's apartment and demanded, "Why didn't you tell me about this?"

Kevin told me, "I had expected him to teach me everything about the Christian life and be there for every experience. I needed healthier expectations." Relationships of spiritual help should be based, in other words, on a clear understanding of our hopes and needs.

We have already suggested one area where expectations need definition. We should be clear if we are seeing a partnership as mutual mentoring and friendship between peers or one of a wiser (perhaps older) guide helping someone needing specific guidance. If we are not clear, it can happen, as it did with my friend Louise, that the younger person will develop feelings of friendship that are not reciprocated by the elder partner. Louise was devastated to learn after several months that her mentor did not consider her to be in his circle of personal friends. He cared about her and wanted to share his wisdom but was not looking for the intimacy of friendship. Similarly, if you are looking for a helper who will give primary focus to you and your needs, be clear that you are asking for that.

And you and your partner should discuss expectations for how long you keep meeting. From the outset Kevin and I openly discussed that our weekly meetings would go for a specified time—six weeks—at which time we would evaluate. Either of us could quit then, and we would still be friends. You may want to settle on a similar, or perhaps longer, time. At that point, you can always extend your friendship or mentoring, as Kevin and I did.

Church leaders Paul Stanley and Robert Clinton wisely talk about *life cycles* of mentoring: "When you enter a mentoring relationship, do not expect it to last forever." They suggest planning periodic points for evaluation and times when either can "back out without losing face. . . . Better to have short periods, evaluation, and closure points with the possibility of reentry than have a sour relationship for a long time that each fears terminating."[1]

Kevin and I also found it crucial to talk openly about what we expected from our weekly meetings. We made it clear that we saw this as a relationship of mutual mentoring; one would not look to the other as a parent or answer-giver. Neither was looking to the other for intensive analysis or in-depth counseling; we were there simply to support and help each other grow spiritually. At the beginning we even said, "No advice given unless asked for."

But while neither was to be the other's therapist, we were also more than friends who got together to relax or have fun (even though that too developed); there was an intentional focus to our friendship that had to do with spiritual growth and accountability.

Gary and Rob had a similar approach when they began to meet regularly. They had spent time together jogging, playing racquetball, and just walking. When each discovered that the other could be relied upon as a sounding board, they began talking about their spiritual journeys and longings. "Then one fall afternoon while walking around a lake, we decided we would try something: Once a week we would get together just to talk about 'our highest ideals and our deepest needs.' And we would pray for each other as often as possible, preferably daily."

But they also wisely decided to be clear about what that would mean. They established from the outset, for example, that neither would feel pressure to share more than he felt comfortable talking about. "We weren't each other's therapists," reflected Gary, "but rather friends who would help each other in the spiritual life. We wouldn't try to change the other person but would work together on changing ourselves."[2] They were clear that they would be mutual mentors and were direct about the goals of their friendship.

On the other hand, "If," as Tilden Edwards says, "you have never been in a serious spiritual friendship before, and your own sense of spiritual life and experience seems thin, then you probably have little spiritual self-confidence and much vulnerability in approaching such a relationship."[3] You will be looking to the other to provide insight and direction. That needs to be made clear.

A final point: Expectations for confidentiality need careful definition. At the beginning, Kevin and I verbally clarified to one another that, other than talking with our wives, the struggles we shared were between the two of us. This kind of safety and clarity allows for an honesty not otherwise possible. It also reminds us both that what we hear from the other is a gift not to be profaned by others who might not understand or care.

STAY ALERT

Distraction may be one of the biggest obstacles to spiritual growth in our busy, sometimes cluttered, lives. Because I get caught up in life's routine, I sometimes let important experiences roll by without really watching or learning from them. The same approach can diminish the good we gain from a spiritual helper. We can just "get through" our times together, never allowing discussion to dip below the surface. We can be presented with a world of insight, but by our inattention miss its life-changing potential.

For one thing, we may miss God's activity in our lives if it is not dramatic. We may dismiss something our spiritual friend tells us because it is plain and near at hand. In this we are like Naaman the leper in the Hebrew scriptures. A Syrian general, he came to the prophet Elisha to be healed. But once he reached the door of Elisha's house, the prophet sent a messenger to say to him, "Go, wash in the Jordan seven times, and your flesh shall be restored and you shall be clean" (2 Kings 5:10). Naaman's initial response was anger: "I thought that for me he [Elisha] would surely come out, and stand and call on the name of the Lord his God, and would wave his hand over the spot, and cure the leprosy! Are not Abana and Pharpar, the rivers of Damascus, better than all the waters of Israel? Could I not wash in them, and be clean?" He turned and went away in a rage (2 Kings 5:11-12).

We are sometimes likewise prone to ignore the simple insight or unornamented truth. But growing in grace involves everyday, not just mountaintop experiences. As Thomas Merton writes, after reading the lives of highly committed and holy people, "some people become convinced that the [spiritual] life must be something like a Wagnerian opera. Tremendous things keep happening all the time. Every new motion of the spirit is heralded by thunder and lightning."[4]

Working on *The Saints among Us*, a book about American religious commitment I cowrote with George Gallup, Jr., I found that deeply spiritual people usually must maintain their spiritual orientation through long stretches of ordinary, mundane experiences. Some had dramatic experiences of the Lord's presence, of course, but others were like one "saint" we interviewed who said, "I haven't had any major visions. I feel God works daily in my life, I talk with him, and I feel he communicates with me, but in terms of a single instance where he 'wrote on the wall,' no." When asked if she had ever had a dramatic religious experience, another saint remarked, "It's not so much in one particular experience, but in looking back over the years, and how situations have ended, you know it didn't happen by chance. More than anything really dramatic, I can see there was a plan there."[5] A spiritual helper can help us see that when we might otherwise miss it.

The seventeenth-century monk Brother Lawrence, known for his *The Practice of the Presence of God*, was able to sense God as deeply while washing the pots and pans as in worship. "The time of business does not with me differ from the time of prayer; and in the noise and clatter of my kitchen, while several persons are at the same time calling for different things, I possess God in as great tranquility as if I were upon my knees at the blessed sacrament."[6]

We need to be patient when dealing with the raw material of our lives. And we need to stay alert to what our spiritual friend may help us see that we might pass over as insignificant. The everyday round of the most "ordinary" life provides every friendship with rich material for discussion and prayer. And if we are spiritually open, we stand to learn much from the interchange.

UNLEARN AND LEAVE BEHIND

We also need to bring openness to another's perspective. This is not so difficult when I'm tired of struggling with a persistent problem on my own and feel driven to ask for help. But when I am not facing a crisis, I may hesitate. My spiritual laziness may make me settle for spiritual mediocrity and keep me from reaching out for something better.

We may even defend well-worn but skewed pictures of who God is and what God is like. Our childhood's Sunday-school conceptions of God may not support the weight of adult pressures and questions, but we may still hesitate to be challenged by another.

"A spiritual friend," says James Houston, "is someone with whom it is safe to take apart our shallow faith, our compulsive addictions, or whatever else might be under the surface of our visible lives. He or she will help us to

We need to be patient when dealing with the raw material of our lives. And we need to stay alert to what our spiritual friend may help us see that we might pass over as insignificant.

exchange our weaknesses for a new source of trust, conviction and desire that will help us to grow spiritually. We have been born into and have grown up in a culture which is deeply alienated from God. So as we cross the border into God's kingdom, with its radically new attitudes and priorities, we will need all the help we can get from a spiritual friend who has made the same perilous journey before."[7]

Over the years, I have discovered within myself a tendency to become self-critical when I fail to do something perfectly. My longing for perfection has not only brought extra pressures to daily relationships; it has also colored my image of God. My mentor of some time ago once pointed this out, gently reminding me that I was too hard on myself when it came to prayer, that I needed to relax more in God's presence and truly enjoy God.

As comforting and reassuring as her message could have sounded, I resisted it. I preferred instead to see myself as a radical Christian, a spiritual athlete in training. And when another friend suggested in a different way, some weeks later, that I needed to rest more in God's promise of acceptance, to receive what God wanted to give as a gift, it became increasingly difficult for me to deny what my mentor had been saying about my approach to prayer.

A spiritual friend may help in another way. He or she may help us through adult "passages" in life—milestones such as marrying, having children, retiring. These can be times of true insight and change, if we are open to discovering new things about ourselves and our lives. We may make significant spiritual discoveries. Especially in the middle and later years of life, our spiritual life may have a more sober quality to it than that of young adulthood. As we face anew issues of identity, career goals, financial security, mortality, and marriage stability, a friend may keep us on track, if we are willing to listen.

A spiritual helper can also shed new light on the content of our praying and keep us from seeing prayer as just asking for personal blessings.

A spiritual helper can also shed new light on the content of our praying and keep us from seeing prayer as just asking for personal blessings. Our devotional life needs a wide range of praise to God, confession of sin, intercession for others, and thanksgiving for answers and blessings received. We need times of talking to God but also restful listening. We need the balancing of Bible study and may need experiences of corporate prayer. Or perhaps keeping a spiritual journal, in which we record reflections on life's happenings and God's doings, may enrich our spiritual life. Whatever we do, a wise friend can be a teacher who reminds us of the rich diversity of Christian praying, who encourages us to stretch our spiritual muscles in varied forms of spiritual discipline. He or she may suggest we read a helpful book on prayer and spiritual practice. We need to be open!

A guide may even suggest a pattern or outline of prayer for us to practice. This helps us not to get stuck on only one or two ways of cultivating the spiritual life. Beth and Sherry agreed to read daily scripture readings from their denomination's prayer book; they would come together each week and share what had struck each of them from the scripture readings. Others will work their way through a devotional book. We may need rounding out in the areas of worship, scripture study and reflection, or prayerful concern for the needs of the world. Another's strengths in such areas can make all the difference.

A friend or guide's help need not be limited to what is said and taught, either. The practice of praying with another for ten minutes at the end (or beginning) of a meeting may do as much to mold and shape our prayer, if we observe our friend's example, as spending an hour talking *about* prayer.

STAY HONEST

If progress comes when I stay open to another's new insight, it also comes when I am honest about my questions or objections. Few things muddle a relationship more than unspoken reservations and secret disagreements. When our friend or mentor makes a comment that challenges us, we should not smile in outward agreement if inwardly we don't. Keeping true feelings hidden prevents the honest interchange that can lead to fresh insight.

We must find the courage to speak what we really are feeling. Otherwise, we say what we *imagine* we should feel or desire. We give a misleading impression. "This," says Thomas Merton, "for all our good intentions, is plain hypocrisy." The result is a web of conversation "spun out of jargon and pious phrases which we have lifted from books and sermons and with which we conceal, rather than reveal, what is in us."[8]

We need, then, to disagree openly sometimes. Only then can spiritual friendship address our true selves. With our defenses and objections out on the table, they can be examined for what they are. And we may find that our guide or friend has misunderstood something we have said; our honest reaction will ensure that the full picture comes into view and that his or her suggestions hit the mark.

I have long struggled to be more frequent and constant in my times of prayer. One time, I remember, I was finding it particularly difficult to wake up early enough every morning to have a consistent prayer time before work. My spiritual mentor at the time encouraged me not to worry. Throughout the week, she told me, find "pools of prime time": a half-hour here, two hours there, when I can withdraw from daily routine and pray. Her advice helped me not get locked into a limiting pattern, but as I experimented, I discovered that I am a morning person who does best getting an early start on things—including prayer. So I argued a bit. "I need to start my day with prayer," I told her. And out of our honest interchange, I came to appreciate both her freeing word of grace and my unique spiritual needs.

It is important to note, however, that honesty requires an atmosphere of trust. This may—and should—take time to build. We do not share our darkest secrets or our most tenacious doubts with everyone. But growing honesty should characterize any relationship that we look to for significant help. That means taking the risks of self-disclosure, taking off the masks that we use to hide our hurts and needs.

ATTEND TO THE UNSEEN HELPER

Perhaps nothing is as important to the success of spiritual friendship as prayer. The underlying source of any growth is not ourselves or our helpers but God.

I once saw a poster that showed two people looking heavenward, with the caption, "Love is not two people looking at each other, but two people looking in the same direction." The same can be said about spiritual partnership. The focus is always ultimately beyond the two involved. In spiritual friendship, it is not enough that each listens to the other; both must listen to God. Listening is a waiting together on God. Paul once told the Colossians that Epaphras "is always wrestling in his prayers on your behalf" (Col. 4:12).

We need that kind of commitment to pray for one another in spiritual friendship, as my friends Esther and Joyce once discovered. When they began meeting, they promised to pray daily for each other. Over a period of several days shortly after they began, Esther found Joyce coming to her mind unusually often. Finally Esther called Joyce, only to hear Joyce confirm that she was in the throes of making a heavy decision. They concluded with a touch of wonder that it must have been the Lord who prompted Esther's stepped-up praying.

We pray, then, not only for our own growth but for our helper's. This need not be an onerous task. The Holy Spirit, who is a helper and guide, can be trusted to prompt us. One man once said, "It is amazing how often the Lord will bring my partner to mind. I believe it's the Holy Spirit's way of honoring our commitment to pray for one another."

This spiritual dimension of friendship should never mean that we grow dependent upon our partner, however. We do not ask them to do for us what God would have us do for ourselves. It can't be a substitute for a daily life with God.

My friend Kevin compares the situation to private music lessons. "When I took oboe and would not practice during the week but play only during the lesson, I hardly improved at all. The only time you play your instrument can't be during the lesson." Nor can the only time we work on spiritual growth and prayer be with our friend.

KEEP GOING

Determination is another key to making the relationship work. Even clarifying expectations and having a "trial" time does not mean that tough issues won't surface later in the relationship. Any intimate relationship will inevitably involve tense moments. Exposing one's deepest thoughts and longings opens up many opportunities for misunderstanding.

During such difficult times, I may feel tempted to give up and find another friend or mentor. As we will see in the next chapter, sometimes change is indeed warranted. But often growth comes only at those uncomfortable junctures when we resist the urge to flee from a difficult situation.

In certain religious orders the members take what is known as a vow of stability. This is a commitment on their part to stay in their particular community even when it would be tempting to find another. A kind of vow of stability makes sense for our friendships as well. Our friend may say something that troubles us. We may rebel or react defensively. At such a time we scrutinize our reactions. We may be resisting an insight that could be the catalyst for new growth in grace and truth. We need to stay open. And we should not assume the disagreement or tension automatically means that something is wrong.

On the other hand, discomfort may sometimes signal that your partnership is growing in unhealthy ways. Commitment does not mean staying put in a relationship that has become ailing or ingrown. Consider sharing your concerns with a pastor or wise friend if you need help sorting them out.

As we commit ourselves to a transforming friendship, and as we pray expectantly and openly, we can expect God to use the insights—even the disagreement—to help us become the people we long to be and that God can help us become.

FOR FURTHER REFLECTION

• Read or review the Book of Ruth. Note times when Naomi was a motherly mentor to Ruth. Note how Ruth in turn cared for her mother-in-law. What does this story suggest about God's ability to use everyday circumstances for God's higher glory?

• Consider these safeguards that will minimize misunderstandings as you begin a relationship with a spiritual companion:

Talk over and define expectations with your partner.

1. Discuss such things as frequency of meeting and what will happen during your times together.

2. Discuss your hopes for your meetings. Are they specifically for you and your spiritual growth, or mutual?

3. Establish a set number of meetings, after which you can evaluate, terminate, or renegotiate the relationship. This will avoid awkwardness if needs change or the relationship does not work out and will provide an opportunity for refining the purposes of your meetings.

• Do you agree with James Houston's statement that "we have been born into and grown up in a culture which is deeply alienated from God. So as we cross the border into God's kingdom, with its radically new attitudes and priorities, we will need all the help we can get from a spiritual friend"? Does his statement imply that growth often comes at the expense of old patterns of believing? What might that mean for you?

• Think of a time when a discovery forced you to revise your opinion of someone. Or recall a moment when you learned that a long-held prejudice was baseless. Why does it often seem frightening to change? How might such fear affect our openness to the new perspective of a spiritual helper?

• Recall a time when a friend or loved one confronted you with a hard truth about yourself. How did you react? What would you do differently now?

• Begin praying for your own spiritual growth. If you have a helper or friend, begin praying daily for him or her, and for a growing deepening relationship. Your prayers need not be elaborate, just heartfelt.

A FIGHT IN THE EARLY CHURCH

Not every mentoring relationship in the Bible was smooth going. Take the case of Paul and John Mark.

John Mark was, we learn in Acts 12:25, a companion on Paul and Barnabas's preaching mission in Asia Minor. But for reasons unnoted, John Mark left them midjourney to return to Jerusalem (Acts 13:13). Homesickness for Jerusalem, altered travel plans prompted by an illness of Paul's, and a change in leadership from Barnabas to Paul have all been suggested as explanations. Whatever the reason, Paul was upset at this young colleague. Speaking of a later missionary trip, Acts tells us "Barnabas wanted to take with them John called Mark. But Paul decided not to take with them one who had deserted them in Pamphylia and had not accompanied them in the work. The disagreement became so sharp that they parted company" (Acts 15:37-39).

The two eventually were able to resume their relationship, however. Paul tells the church at Colossae, "Mark the cousin of Barnabas, concerning whom you have received instructions—if he comes to you, welcome him" (Col. 4:10). Paul even told Timothy, "Get Mark and bring him with you, for he is useful in my ministry" (2 Tim. 4:11). A mentoring relationship that saw brokenness and pain became, through the working of God's grace, a renewed partnership in learning and ministry—so much so that John Mark was most likely the Mark who wrote one of the New Testament's four Gospels, the one that bears his name. ∾

SEVEN

When It's Time to Move On

Make no friends with those given to anger,
and do not associate with hotheads,
or you may learn their ways
and entangle yourself in a snare.

Proverbs 22:24-25

The soul must . . . without concern for others' opinions, go
freely where it finds its best director, going where God inspires it
to go, and giving the new encounter every benefit.
Jean Joseph Surrin, Seventeenth-Century French Christian

⸎

S ome years ago, during the time of transition after my
move to a Chicago suburb, I felt something was missing. I had friends at the office and in my church, but I
missed having someone to talk to about deeper spiritual
questions. There was no spiritual crisis—I was praying most
mornings and found personal Bible study meaningful. But
I still needed something, someone. I wanted more support
and guidance. Having read about the church's tradition of
"spiritual directors," I assumed a director was what I
needed. But who?

I asked a coworker who I thought would know about
such things. He gave me the name of a Catholic retreat

center that had several spiritual directors in residence. I made contact and was given someone's name. With some trepidation, I called and talked with a warm, sensible-sounding woman. We scheduled an appointment, and I began meeting with Marjorie every six weeks or so. Marjorie was a middle-aged nun who made me feel comfortable from the first moment I sat in her simply appointed office.

I still recall the rested feeling I had as I crossed the parking lot to enter the retreat center, set in quiet woods, which I could see through a large window in Marjorie's office. More than once I thought, *What a luxury!* To be able to spend an hour with another person with no other agenda but to discuss my discoveries and longing in the Christian life—this seemed like a rich gift.

More than once I thought,
What a luxury! *to be able to spend an hour with another person with no other agenda but to discuss my discoveries and longings in the Christian life— this seemed like a rich gift.*

But this was not all I experienced. I began to realize that Marjorie and I had different understandings of prayer—even of God. We both shared a desire to grow in closeness to God, but she seemed uncomfortable with some of my theological convictions, as I was with some of her theology. Besides, my weekly meetings with Kevin, which had been going on for some months, became an increasing source of support and insight for me. While Kevin had no formal training in spiritual guidance, I found that our goals for our Christian lives were similar. His observations were hitting the mark. After consulting with friends and my wife, I decided that my relationship with Kevin deserved my concentration. I thanked my first "official" spiritual director for her help, and I brought our relationship to a cordial close.

Sometimes our attempts to find spiritual friendship do not pan out. Pastor and writer Eugene H. Peterson tells of learning this when he came home for the summer after his second year in college, full of questions about God and spiritual things.

Peterson turned first to his pastor. "After listening to me for about five minutes," he recounts, "he diagnosed my problem as sex, and launched into a rambling exposition on the subject." A second visit shed no more light.

Next Petersom turned to a man in his congregation who had a saintly reputation. Confined to a wheelchair from a gunshot wound decades before, the man was seen often at church, Bible open on his lap. "All the years of my growing up," writes Peterson, "I had heard people say that he was wise and holy." He seemed perfect for spiritual conversation.

But, Peterson remembers, "It turned out there was no conversation. He was only interested in acquiring an audience for his 'wisdom' and proceeded to lecture me interminably from Ephesians for the three or four meetings that I had with him."

A friend finally suggested that Peterson see Reuben Lance, a gruff village character with a wild red beard, a jack-of-all-trades who was an "expert in everything manual: carpentry, plumbing, electrical work, masonry." Reuben Lance, says Peterson, "treated my God interest, my prayer hunger, with great dignity." Through unassuming, prayerful conversation, Reuben brought Peterson to a new understanding of God and God's work in his life.[1]

We will not, then, always find the right mentor or friend at first crack. How do we know if we should end what we have begun? And what do we do when we conclude it's time to move on?

REASONS TO QUIT

A friend once told me of his efforts to meet with a spiritual helper and friend. While he started out with high hopes, his friend was a person who "covered up his emotions," making for what at times seemed an impenetrable wall. "Week after week I would ask him, 'How's it going?' His answer was always 'Fine.' But I knew from others who were close to him that things were not always fine. I would share some of my struggles, and we would pray together, but he couldn't seem to bring himself to share those places in his life that needed help."

When their trial period of six weeks was over, the two men agreed to stop meeting. "It was hard to say, 'This isn't working,'" my friend recalls. "It was awkward, but there comes a time when you have to say, 'It's time to quit.' We realized things just were not going to click." Sometimes personalities don't mesh, or one partner has a different agenda than the other. We may find that the person we sought out has psychological problems that keep him or her from being of help to us.

Or we may find that theological differences emerge that require too much energy and time defending. A charismatic might run into difficulty with a staunch Wesleyan, for example, just as a liturgical Lutheran might not hit it off with a fundamentalist Baptist. While such pairing could lead to great enrichment, such differences may distract from the primary task of listening to each other and praying together.

Or, as we mature, we may find that a companion that seemed tailor-made for us at one stage in life becomes less beneficial at another. My friend Susan had a spiritual mentor who taught her a tremendous amount about keeping a journal, relating to friends, and listening for God's guidance. But when Susan found herself in a rocky romantic relationship that needed a clean break, she found her mentor's temperament so different that she could not gain much support from her. Because it was such a huge issue for Susan at the time, she could not talk about her spiritual life without reference to her disintegrating romance. She could not expect from her spiritual mentor the same insight in this area that she had in others, and she had to find another friend for a sounding board.

Leaving a job or moving to another part of the country may also dictate a conclusion or redefinition of the relationship. "I started school and left the area," Susan explained to me about a later stage in her relationship to her spiritual mentor. "We still keep in touch, but not as intensely as before. I touch base with her when facing major obstacles, decisions, and joys." Susan feels her friend will "always be there for me," but the relationship has taken on a different quality due to geographical distance.

Finally, friendships sometimes simply go sour. Perhaps we project too many expectations upon our friend. Maybe misunderstanding creeps in due to our inattention. Or competitiveness and jealousy may taint our meetings. The psalmist complains about a friend's treachery, "It is not enemies who taunt me—I could bear that; it is not adversaries who deal insolently with me—I could hide from them. But it is you, my equal, my companion, my familiar friend, with whom I kept pleasant company; we walked in the house of God with the throng" (Ps. 55:12-14). Friendships do not always end pleasantly.

Whatever the reason, there may come a time to move on. Writes the Dutch Christian Pére Yves Ernest Masson, "Although it is best usually to confide in only one [spiritual mentor], there is no need to be so completely attached to him [or her]. One should be sufficiently indifferent in him [or her] in order to be able to do without him [or her]; to be free to consult another, or even to change him [or her] altogether if need be."[2]

What are the concrete steps if you feel it's time to bring a prayer partnership or spiritual mentoring relationship to a close? What do you do if you find yourself restless after times with your spiritual friend, wondering if you have wasted time, or worse, been given inadequate counsel? How can you make a decision based on prudence and wisdom?

GO SLOWLY

First make certain that you are not avoiding painful issues that your friend or director may be raising for your benefit. Sometimes the hardest words to hear produce in us the greatest change and transformation. And even if your helper is clumsy or heavy-handed, there may be a great gift to be had if you humbly listen. And a different personality or theological perspective may do us good. For all the extra energy required to relate to someone who irritates us occasionally, God may have our growth in view.

We should remember too that there is no such thing as a perfect friend or mentor. Even the most sanctified and sensitive spiritual guide can miss responding to the nuances of our life's struggles and joys. This is all the more likely if we have not been open and honest with our companion or have not given him or her sufficient time to truly get to know us. We may need to adjust our expectations or even find complementary help from another. But that does not mean we break off meeting.

Indeed, leaving out of personal discomfort or because we want to avoid conflict may catch up with us later. We may simply repeat our failed encounter—always avoiding, never resolving, the issues that keep us from deep and transforming encounters with God and others. So we should not be hasty or haphazard.

SEEK COUNSEL

When I was thinking about bringing my relationship with Marjorie, my first director, to a close, I found feedback from others invaluable. Talking through my decision allowed me to check that my motives were solid, that I wasn't just trying to evade significant issues important to my growth. I realized more fully through talking with others that my gentle restlessness, was simply due to a difference in our understandings of God and prayer. I respected Marjorie but needed something else.

I also found that the input of others allowed me to be more confident and self-assured about my decision when I did decide to stop meeting with Marjorie. It can be awkward to bow out of something two people entered with high hopes, and it may require support.

TAKE COURAGE

It is difficult to end or break off a relationship that we enter with high expectations. Not only may we feel some grief, but there is always the risk that our partner will be hurt or will misunderstand. We may fear that we will seem ungrateful, or that our ending a relationship suggests we think ourselves somehow better than the other. But the risk is worth taking if the relationship has stopped being helpful.

"Life both changes and needs change," writes Isabel Anders, "and our friends are as human and flawed as we are. . . . Friendship can falter at any stage for lack of watering or nurturing, for neglecting to truly listen to the other. It can range from cutting off a potential act of caring, refusing to meet, in kind, an extension of the other's hopes and fears—to encompass a wide range of betrayal and abuse of confidences."[3]

If it is we who initiate the withdrawal or redefinition, the likelihood of our hurting our mentor or friend can be mitigated by our approach. Simple honesty, combined with expressions of appreciation for what we learned, can help a break be clean and uncluttered. We should guard, for example, against subterfuge and excuse making (for example, "Forty-five minutes is really too far for me to drive every month to get together with you"). Yet neither do we have to be bluntly unkind. Not only is sharpness needlessly hurtful, months (or years) later we may see in clearer light the wisdom of a director whose care is not to our liking right now. Humility is always in order.

And we will likely find that our friend or director understands our need for a change. Centuries ago, John of the Cross, a great Spanish spiritual director, wrote,

> Spiritual directors should give freedom to people and support them in their desire to seek growth. The director does not know the means by which God may wish to honor a soul, especially if that soul is no longer satisfied with the director's counsel. This dissatisfaction is indeed a clear sign that the director is not helping the soul. . . . These directors should themselves advise people to change. To do otherwise comes from foolish pride and possessiveness or some other personal need.[4]

We may also consider getting together more informally and infrequently, even after we stop meeting regularly. Especially in the case of a friendship, the characteristics that attracted you in the first place can continue to be a part of your life, only now in a less-defined way.

END WELL

One of the ten commandments of mentoring relationships, say Christian leaders Paul Stanley and Robert Clinton, is "Bring closure to the mentoring relationship." When this happens successfully, the result is often "an ongoing friendship that allows for occasional mentoring and future interweaving of lives as needed."[5]

Ending well is unfortunately not something that happens naturally. It takes work and may require some risks. But it is far better—for you and for your partner—than letting things trail off to nothing but uneasy, unresolved feelings.

When Karen left her church and thereby felt compelled to end the mentoring relationship she enjoyed with her pastor, she found it valuable to be open: "We said, 'It's time to part ways.' I affirmed all he had done. Then we had a time of prayer where we 'released' one another in the Spirit."

TAKE HOPE

When a friendship does not work out, the temptation is to conclude that it cannot *ever* work out. Instead, we need to learn from our experiences and trust that we will enter the next friendship or mentorship wiser and all the more ready to learn and give to one another.

Just as prayer for God's help and guidance is important in seeking and finding a guide, it is equally important in ending a relationship. Francis de Sales, the early-seventeenth-century French bishop, once wrote to a person in his care,

> Since it is of the greatest urgency, Philothea, that you should travel with a good guide on this holy journey of sanctity, pray to God with great zeal, to provide you with a person after the heart of God, and have no doubt; for even though God should have to send an angel from heaven, . . . he will give you a guide who is good and faithful. . . . I say once more to you, pray to God to give you such a person, and, when you have received him, praise his divine Majesty, remain steadfast and do not search for any other, but travel on simply, humbly, and trustfully, for you will have a most beneficial journey.[6]

FOR FURTHER REFLECTION

• Read Psalm 55. What seems to be the context for the "anguish within" that David describes in verse 4? In what ways has a friend's hurtful actions prompted the heartache and fear David describes? Note that some commentators suggest that the situation is like that of Absalom's conspiracy against the king in 2 Samuel 15-17.

• Think of an occasion when a friend or mentor challenged you to take a new perspective. How did your reaction further or hinder your personal growth? Was the criticism fair? How did you know? What did you learn from the experience about coping with those who lovingly confront you?

• List the people you could talk to if you began to suspect your spiritual helper is not right for you. How might their varied perspectives keep you from a hasty or unwise decision or give you courage to quit?

• What issues could become a problem in your relationship with your spiritual mentor? What might you need to do to ensure that areas of difference do not grow into areas of conflict?

• Set up a time with your helper to evaluate the relationship. Be sure to affirm his or her strengths. Talk also about how the relationship can continue to be the best that it can be for both of you. Plan to have regular times of evaluation and reassessment.

THE APOSTLE ALMOST NOBODY REMEMBERS

Of the apostles in the New Testament, Barnabas may be the furthest from being a household name. His colleague Paul, on the other hand, is one of the New Testament's most oft-quoted writers. But it wasn't always that way. Barnabas at one time had pride of place in the early church. His status now as a veritable unknown disguises the fact that, as much as anyone, he was responsible for the flowering of the impressive gifts and astounding influence of his colleague Paul. Paul would not be who he is today had Barnabas never gotten involved.

Because Paul (at the time still known as Saul) once aggressively persecuted Christians, Acts 9:1-26 tells us, the rest of the apostles kept their distance when Paul came to Jerusalem. It was Barnabas who saw Paul's potential and "brought him to the apostles" (Acts 9:27). He was not put off by this brash convert and "sponsored" him until Paul could prove his conversion. Barnabas must have also spent time with Paul, teaching him, coaching him, and watching as his convictions and remarkable gifts matured.

In Paul's case the *mentored* became a *mentor* to others. That may well have not happened if Barnabas had not poured himself into young Saul. Because he did, Paul's life changed, as did the countless people Paul reached in his own time and in the centuries since. ᴄᴀ❧

EIGHT

When We Reach Out to Others

The love of our neighbor is the only door out of the dungeon of self.

George MacDonald

Whoever walks with the wise becomes wise.

Proverbs 13:20

☙

When young Holden Caulfield of J. D. Salinger's *The Catcher in the Rye* is moved by a crisis to visit a teacher he has loved, the old man assures him, "Many, many men have been just as troubled morally and spiritually as you are right now. Happily, some of them kept records of their troubles. You'll learn from them—if you want to. Just as someday, if you have something to offer, someone will learn something from you. It's a beautiful reciprocal arrangement."[1]

My friend Susan found that her relationship with her mentor became a "beautiful reciprocal arrangement." As her mentor invested hours in helping her learn spiritual disciplines and become more aware of the love of God, Susan naturally began to find within herself "a greater inner strength and a greater confidence to hear the voice of

God." She also began to realize that her relationship to her mentor was "evolving." Now Susan notices new dynamics: "at times she's a friend and at times she's a mentor, and at times I can't tell the difference."

Another friend went to a woman she respected as spiritual and wise. But after a while her mentor said, "I need a mentor in some areas of need in *my* life." Says my friend: "She needed me to be there for her. So she ceased to be my mentor, and I was content to be her friend."

As these accounts show, progress in our spiritual lives may mean we move into a new place of not being merely the receiver. Indeed, a cornerstone of Christian faith is that a full Christian life involves both receiving spiritual blessing and in turn becoming a blessing. We deepen our Christian life for more than our private edification. We grow to help others grow. The one who learns becomes one who helps others learn, in a beautiful reciprocal relationship.

This happens in an ultimate way when we spend time with Christ, of course. "I am the vine, you are the branches. Those who abide in me and I in them bear much fruit. . . . I do not call you servants any longer, because the servant does not know what the master is doing; but I have called you friends, because *I have made known to you* everything that I have heard from my Father" (John 15:5, 15, italics mine). Those who spent time with Christ, those in whom his life and influence had grown, would in turn have a fruitful effect on others.

It should also happen as we spend time with our mentor or friend. This is something of what the apostle Paul had in mind when he wrote to Timothy. While he calls Timothy his "loyal child in the faith," he also writes, "These are the things [that you learned from me and others] you must insist on and teach. Let no one despise your youth, but set the believers an example in speech and conduct, in love, in faith, in purity," (1 Tim. 1:2; 4:11-12).

I saw from the mentor's side how this can happen. Several years ago, when I lived in Virginia, a young friend joined me in what soon became a "reciprocal relationship." A high-school senior, Ben was wondering about Christianity, which he had briefly rebelled against. He showed up at my church one Sunday and went out of his way to talk with me about his spiritual questions.

Then Ben attended a large regional youth conference. One of the workshop leaders encouraged him to meet with someone regularly for Bible study. Ben returned from his meeting and asked if we could get together once a week.

Progress in our spiritual lives may mean we move into a new place of not being merely the receiver. Indeed, a cornerstone of Christian faith is that a full Christian life involves both receiving spiritual blessing and in turn becoming a blessing. . . . The one who learns becomes one who helps others learn, in a beautiful reciprocal relationship.

As we met, I found that Ben had the springtime faith of a new convert. His enthusiasm needed grounding and maturing, but his eagerness was contagious—especially when it came to prayer. Unbothered by the finer points of theology, he simply wanted to experience as much of God's presence and power as he could. I found my own longing for a deeper experience of prayer challenged and encouraged by Ben's exuberance.

Driving alone in my car one February afternoon, shortly after we had begun meeting, I experienced a breakthrough in my praying. Ben's example had been deepening *my* hunger for more of God. As I drove I uncovered a longed-for intensity in praise and communion not bound by words. The experience brought a depth and fluency in praying that has rarely been far from me ever since. My young friend, who *I* was supposed to help, was the catalyst for my own growth. While he was the younger and less spiritually mature, God used him in my life, as God seems often to use those who follow.

As we try to help another, sometimes God uses us through surprisingly simple means. Richard J. Foster notes,

> One day I had a strong feeling to call a parishioner who is a college chaplain. I said, "John, I didn't call you to ask you to do anything. I just wanted to say 'Hi.'" On the other end there was a deep sigh of relief and he said, "I'm so glad you called." Then he began to share a deep inner need. So often love is communicated not in the big event, but in small acts of kindness. One of the greatest expressions of love is simply to notice people and pay attention to them.[2]

We may picture ministry as the domain of the professionally religious, taking place only in a pulpit or pastor's study. But far more ministry happens through everyday people than the few who serve the church full-time.

A friend once told me, "I was thinking about the things people have done for me through my life that meant the most to me. I realized it was the almost unplanned, tiny touches—the small gifts, like picking up a phone to ask how I'm doing—that mattered the most. Often it was the Holy Spirit prompting them to do the small thing, but it was the right thing at the right time, and it had great significance."

God has chosen, according to the J. B. Phillips translation of 1 Corinthians 1:28, "things of little strength and

A friend once told me, "I was thinking about the things people have done for me through my life that meant the most to me. I realized it was the almost unplanned, tiny touches—— the small gifts, like picking up a phone to ask how I'm doing—— that mattered the most."

small repute . . . to explode the pretensions of the things that are." God often calls on ordinary, "little" people to do quietly extraordinary things.

I find a phrase of church leaders Paul Stanley and Robert Clinton helpful. They talk about "one anothering," referring to the many times in the New Testament that Christians are appointed to do things for "one another": "Love one another," we read in John 13:34-35 and 1 John 3:11; "Bear with one another and, if anyone has a complaint against another, forgive each other," Colossians 3:13 says. We read in Hebrews about provoking "one another to love and good deeds" (10:24). James says, "Confess your sins to one another, and pray for one another, so that you may be healed" (James 5:16). Stanley and Clinton ask, "Why is 'one anothering' missing from Christian fellowships?"[3] These activities do not require great experience. There is no reason we cannot begin practicing them in small and everyday ways, and people around us will be helped.

Sometimes all it takes is alert sensitivity on our parts. I found that out with George, another friend. He would drive home from work on the road that curved around the front of my house. Sometimes, if I was in the yard, he would stop and talk. We would stand under the shade of two huge maples whose branches interlocked overhead, talking about his job, our young children, or the intricate web of extended family relationships at the church we attended.

One time, as I leaned against one of the trunks, I shared with him the progress I was making in my practice of prayer after getting to know Ben. George responded with wistfulness. For all his years of church attendance, he told me, he was bored and "flustrated" with his Christian life. "I feel like I have been studying Sunday school lessons for years," he confessed, "but never seem to get anywhere. Lately I've gotten away from praying. And when I do pray, I have trouble knowing the words to say. I sometimes pile up big, theological-sounding words, so my prayers sound spiritual."

I cannot remember what I said in response, but I have never forgotten how I immediately sensed I was witnessing a time of profound spiritual openness in a friend's life. Because of my sharing and listening, we were able to explore together an area of great need and spiritual opportunity.

In our society, it seems, much nurturing is impromptu; spiritual direction sometimes takes place on the run. Riding together in the car, someone may start telling you about their interest in attending church. Or somebody pulls you aside after a meeting, passes you in the hall, approaches you in the parking lot. People are constantly verbalizing concerns that are ultimately spiritual in character, even if they mask them.

When someone says, "Think about me" on their way into surgery, it usually means, "I need you to pray for me." When a friend confides anxiety to us about being able to pay the bills, there is frequently an unspoken, unarticulated theological dimension (learning to trust). If you are attentive, you can help someone. And it may set the stage for a deeper relationship.

Whether we ever help others in an "official" capacity or not, we can always be open to involving ourselves in others' spiritual concerns in a supportive way.

HELPING OUR HELPER

If we have a mentor, this movement into a helping mode may happen in the relationship itself. Even though we have been the student, we may find a relationship of increasing equality and mutuality. You and your partner may become colleagues, able to support and help each other. "The further the 'disciple' progresses," writes spiritual director Josef Sudbrack, "the more the 'master' must withdraw from the center for attention, must become not a 'master' but a 'companion' and even a 'disciple' himself."[4]

In fact, we should beware of becoming so dependent we never grow within the relationship. Susan told me of her mentor, "She let me into her life to see the humanness of it. It would have been easy to exalt her at times because of how God used her in my life, but I've had enough experience in the last several years to respect the 'humanness' factor. There were times I saw her tired, stretched, hurried, or when the words of feedback didn't hit their mark. And as I have grown and changed, she has started to receive from me as well." The dynamics began to change.

If, however, your helper has many more years of maturity and experience, you may find the relationship always and inevitably that of leader and learner, mentor and protégé. Sometimes the relationship never develops much mutuality, and the outlet for our sharing will involve others we know or meet. We can be assured, however, that God will find ways to touch people and accomplish God's will through us.

TRYING YOUR WINGS

What if you feel you have something to share with another and want to "graduate" to being a mutual mentor to someone else?

We need first to remember that less important than an aptitude for counseling is our willingness to be used of God in listening, praying with, and walking alongside. Awareness of psychological dynamics can be valuable, of course; some spiritual problems grow out of emotional scars. But even without training, you can offer something valuable to another. Despite the "professionalization" of our culture, where it is assumed that only experts or specialists can help, our gift of prayerful friendship is no small offering. Your willingness to share yourself—through encouragement and a commitment to pray—may help someone in a quiet way that only you can perform.

While my friend Karen learned a great deal from her pastor and mentor, the relationship began to take on a new character. "The relationship was more one-way at the beginning. He was building me up through prayer and his example and things he said. After a while it became more mutual. He would begin to open up and share things with me for prayer." She took on a significant ministry of prayer for her mentor.

THE BLIND LEADING THE BLIND?

In a relationship of mutual mentoring, some areas need special consideration.

First, you may not feel the security you did from getting direction from an "old saint." Your mutual relationship may feel more like the "blind leading the blind." Occasionally you may both run into problems that neither of you seems to be able to shed much light on.

In some areas, in other words, your partner's presence and willingness to pray will not be enough. Or your less-experienced companion in mutual mentoring may not have learned the importance of patient, painstaking listening. He or she may be too quick to offer advice. He or she may misread what you are saying and provide counsel not based on complete understanding. A friend may also suggest a wrong turn or be too tentative—less able, because of lack of confidence, to confront you when you are contemplating a misstep.

In addition, if we come to experience a time of upheaval in our personal or spiritual lives, a mutual helping relationship may not provide the same time and attention that a relationship with a spiritual director might. Because our partner also looks to us for support, we will not feel free to focus as much attention on our own needs even when they are acute.

SHARING IN THE DEPTHS

There are also a number of ways your mutual mentoring of someone will provide great benefits to you and him or her.

We can usually learn and grow from hearing the struggles of another, for example. One man who had been in a relationship of mutual helping learned a lot about his own faith by watching his partner struggle with financial priorities. He told his friend, "The whole area of Christian giving was new to me. But I heard you talk consistently about giving generously, even when it wasn't easy. And when I know that I will see you regularly, it helps me feel more accountable when I face major purchases." Like my friend, we may sharpen our perception of how God works by observing God's action in the daily moments of a mutual mentor's life.

Also, a relationship of mutual helping can keep us from becoming too inwardly focused, too caught up in every fleeting moment of doubt, too absorbed by the workings of our own spiritual life. Spirituality should always strengthen us for the battle of faith, not encourage a retreat into an insulated, isolated inner world. Helping another reminds us that the goal of Christian growth is greater than our own warm feeling. It reminds us that God cares deeply about a whole world of people. It makes it easier to remember that what we gain from our spiritual life is more than private fulfillment. Our growth should be shared with others.

Finally, many find that what they give away in ministry to others, far from draining them, revitalizes their faith. And what they attempt to teach and pass along to others becomes embedded in their minds like no other lessons can. Such a feeling of gratification is not the basis of our getting involved in another's life, but it is often a blessed outcome. Whatever form it takes, drawing alongside another to help is full of both risks and promise. The next two chapters offer guidance to help you avoid some detours and wrong turns and brave the road ahead with more competence and confidence.

Spirituality should always strengthen us for the battle of faith, not encourage a retreat into an insulated, isolated inner world. Helping another reminds us that the goal of Christian growth is greater than our own warm feelings. It reminds us that God cares deeply about a whole world of people.

FOR FURTHER REFLECTION

• Read Acts 9:19-30. What do we learn about Barnabas's "mentoring" role with the then-young Christian Saul? How did it make a difference? (See also Acts 13:1-3.)

• What signs of growth might indicate to you that you are ready to do more than just receive from another—but to pass insight or support on to others?

• Do you agree with the warning in this chapter that we should beware of becoming so dependent on a spiritual mentor that "we never grow in the relationship, never mature to the place where we can help others"? In your relationship with your spiritual helper, how great is this danger?

• What are some avenues already open for you to begin sharing the benefits of your spiritual maturity with others? Whom do you know that might benefit, for example, from your gentle encouragement, or your being available to discuss spiritual issues or your promise that you will pray for them? What obstacles might keep these encounters from taking place? What can you do to overcome them?

• Review the advantages and disadvantages of a mutual helping relationship. In your mind, what is the greatest advantage? Disadvantage? Do you feel ready to be a mutual mentor or special companion to someone? If not, what kind of maturity do you feel you need to cultivate to make that possible some day?

• If you already have begun to be a helper to someone, take five minutes now to pray for your partner. If you haven't, take five minutes to ask God if someone you know now needs your help, be it in a small way or large.

HOW A PROPHET'S MINISTRY LIVED ON

Few biblical figures were as rugged and intense as Elijah. He confronted the idolatry of his people uncompromisingly, and miracles seemed to follow in his wake. He was a hard act to follow. But Elijah knew that he was no one-man show for God's cause. He began to invest himself in a protégé—Elisha—whom God anointed and used in powerful ways as well.

Elisha's induction as Elijah's "mentoree" really begins with the senior prophet's showdown with Israel's evil royal couple, Ahab and Jezebel, in 1 Kings 18. The story of Elijah's ensuing contest with the prophets of Baal is full of drama. God acts on Elijah's behest to "prove" himself as the one true God. But when a victorious Elijah kills the prophets of Baal, he soon must flee the wrath of Ahab and Jezebel. And it is while a hounded, lonely Elijah stands on a mountain and hears a "gentle whisper" (1 Kings 19:12, NIV) that he learns that God wants him to "anoint" Elisha. (Anointing in the Bible—usually done with oil—symbolized consecration to or divine imbuement for God's service.)

"So [Elijah] . . . ," we read, "found Elisha son of Shaphat, who was plowing. . . . Elijah passed by him and threw his mantle over him," thus designating Elisha as successor (1 Kings 19:19). Elisha finishes his business at home and then "set out and followed Elijah, and became his servant" (1 Kings 19:21). While Elijah began as Elisha's "master" (2 Kings 2:3), the younger's ministry takes on its own force. Like Elijah, Elisha moved into a ministry replete with personal drama, confrontation with idolatry, and miracles, such as raising a child from the dead, just as Elijah had done at Zarephath (see 1 Kings 17:8-24 and 2 Kings 4:8-37).

Just before Elijah is to leave the younger prophet for good, Elisha makes a startling request: "Please let me inherit a double share of your spirit."

Elijah hesitates. "You have asked a hard thing," he says. Elijah knows that the answer to Elisha's request was in the Lord's sovereign hands, not his own. So he concluded, "If you see me as I am being taken from you, it will be granted you; if not, it will not." Elijah leaves, Elisha sees, and "when the company of prophets who were at Jericho saw him at a distance, they declared, 'The spirit of Elijah rests on Elisha' " (2 Kings 2:9-10, 15). ᎣᏩ

NINE

When Someone Seeks Your Help

One of the great rewards of loving God is being able to love others who also love [God].

Saint-Evremond

A brother's miseries [are] truly experienced only by one who has misery in his own heart. You will never have real mercy for the failing of another until you know and realize that you have the same failings in your soul.

Bernard of Clairvaux

Blessed be the God and Father of our Lord Jesus Christ. . . . who consoles us in all our affliction, so that we may be able to console those who are in any affliction with the consolation with which we ourselves are consoled by God.

2 Corinthians 1:3-4

❧

*N*ot long ago Charles went out for breakfast with Bill, a younger friend from his church. Bill had come to Charles often, in fact, with questions about a dating relationship—especially how to sort through whether to get "serious." This morning he also had something else on his mind. Bill had heard Charles talk over the months about his regular prayer partner, and now he wanted to know if Charles would be the same to him. "I know you already meet with someone, but would you consider being my spiritual mentor? I want to develop a prayer life where I learn to 'hear God.'" Bill had begun hungering for the relationship he heard Charles occasionally allude to.

As we learn and grow from the influence of a spiritual helper, as Charles did, we may face similar encounters. People may approach *us* asking for help, just as it happened for writer Avery Brooke. Avery formed a group within her church to work on the church's newsletter/magazine, but the group quickly became a close-knit fellowship where planning for next month's articles mingled with spiritual discussions and prayer for one another's needs. People in the church couldn't help noticing the growth that began to take place. One of us would be talking to a friend about daily happenings or to an author about an article, and the subject would begin to shift," Brooke recalls. Surprisingly probing conversations about spiritual matters—prayer, the nature of God—naturally blossomed between group members and the rest of the congregation. "And suddenly we would find ourselves in a deeper and more personal place than we had expected. Haltingly, we would try to say something of the God we prayed to, of Christ."[1]

As these stories show, the difference that begins to blossom within us will make others take notice and sometimes, perhaps, ask for help. They may even turn to us to be a spiritual mentor. What should we do?

WHEN A FRIEND COMES KNOCKING

To begin with, don't feel that you must take on the responsibility if the thought overwhelms you. You may simply not be equipped for spiritual direction, however much you have grown. Your feelings are strong clues as to whether or not you are ready to guide another. Sometimes deeper insights come only with experience.

Or you may not have a natural facility in relating to others. You may simply not be drawn to the practice. There is no need to feel guilty if you feel more at home sharing yourself through writing, parenting, teaching, behind-the-scenes serving, or helping the physically needy. The ways we help others are as varied as our personalities.

And you may simply not have the time. As it turns out, my friend Charles ended up gently saying no to Bill; he felt that he was so overcommitted in other areas that he could not add another regular meeting.

But what if we're not sure? How do we determine if we should become another's director or guiding friend?

STARTING RIGHT

First, pray. If the goal of spiritual mentoring is deepening a person's relationship with God, and if the wisdom for mentoring is rooted in prayer, the decision whether or not to mentor another should grow out of prayerful reflection. As you pray, do your best to avoid assuming that you should—or shouldn't. Try to stay open, like my friend Karen. A friend asked her one Sunday if she would be her spiritual mentor and prayer partner. "I was so busy in church," Karen remembers, "that I wasn't sure I'd have the time to commit. But I felt I *should.* Amazingly, what I thought was going to be an exhausting, giving time became one of the highlights of the week. I had a love and a compassion for her; God gave me the strength to love her through a hard time."

You even may be surprised at the direction of God's nudge. God sometimes surprises us with leadings; God may have you do something for which you feel little ability (making his power "perfect" in your weakness, to recall Paul's phrase in 2 Cor. 12:9). A healthy amount of anxiety and natural discomfort for taking on a responsibility is normal.

Remember too that you must be motivated by more than good feelings. The care of another's soul is too awesome a responsibility to undertake on a whim or out of an unstudied desire to be merely "useful." God may tell you, "Not yet." Or you may sense a definite "no" for reasons you do not understand at the time. And you must sift and sort to make sure you are not saying yes out of needs to build your ego and feel "important."

CONSIDER WHAT'S INVOLVED

You need also to count the cost. Can you afford time to become involved in someone's spiritual life in an intimate way? Ask yourself where time will come from to meet with someone. Will it rob family time? Cut into personal devotional times? Often helping another with deep issues involves more time than we estimate. I have talked to few people who became involved in a helping way with others who did not find it taking more time than they first thought. And the sense of spiritual responsibility may use up emotional reserves even when we are not directly spending time with someone.

JOIN WITH OTHERS IN DECIDING

Another helpful step in deciding is to enlist the counsel of your own spiritual helper or pastor. If you are part of a small group whose members are accustomed to praying for others' needs, think about asking the group to make it a matter of prayer.

Whatever you do, find someone who knows you well and can ensure that your decision to try to help another is wise. It is too easy to rush to help prematurely or for wrong reasons. Particularly when we are young in faith, still feeling the first flush of spiritual passion, we may not see all the complexities. A green spring bud needs time and growth under the right conditions before it can produce fruit.

WATCHING OTHERS COME

You may also get some sense of direction by noting if others come to you for advice about spiritual matters. If people around you suspect that you can be confided in, if they sense you can share in their joys and struggles, they will turn to you without your campaigning or advertising your wisdom.

The woman mentored by Karen in the story above asked Karen largely because when she approached Karen one Sunday morning for prayer, Karen had what seemed to be a word of encouragement from the Lord. Karen remembers, "She opened up and shared her struggle. The she wanted to know if I could get together with her to pray."

A CONFIDENT YES

Finally, if you have prayed, counted the cost, sought others' counsel, and seen people approach you, say yes humbly but confidently. Assisting another in his or her spiritual growth is both more awesome and more simple than we might think.

I have a friend who has discovered this. "It has really helped me to realize that an important part of what I do is simply to look for what God is already doing in this person's life. This person just didn't appear in my office or on my doorstep. God's already been working. God has created this person and provided a Redeemer for him or her. God has provided a life full of shaping experiences that have brought this individual to this point. My job is to help him or her see what God is already doing, how their current experiences fit into that." That takes pressure off us for having to know and notice everything.

It also means that effective spiritual direction will major on listening to God and listening attentively to the other. That means I am not the focus of what happens. I need to pray, to be wise in the word, and to keep my own prayer life active and growing.

And I must learn to listen. As simple as it is, listening helps others relax. They feel they can finally share what is on their heart, can get doubts into the light, can get questions in the open air of prayerful discussion. When we offer a listening ear, we offer a powerful reminder to others that God listens to them.

So our first questions are not, What am I going to say to this person? Or, How do I keep from saying the wrong thing? Rather, they are What is God saying? and, How can I listen alertly to this person—who he is, what she believes, what causes him struggle? Our primary role is not to provide answers but to listen in a way that helps us and our friend listen for what God is saying. We don't need a license in professional spiritual direction to do so.

We should never hesitate to turn to a wise friend or even a helping professional if we have questions about our mentoring relationship or our partner. We will ourselves need accountability and the clarity and objectivity of another's perspective.

But mostly we need to make ourselves available to others. Do we have the patience and the desire to carefully attend to another's life? The answer to that question matters more than our degrees or years of experience.

The late priest and writer Henri J. M. Nouwen argued that the spiritual helper was not one who has achieved perfection. He used the image of the "wounded healer." A minister, helper, or spiritual friend, in other words, is one who finds the grace to look after the wounds of others, even while he or she continues to be healed.

What is most important is that we be ready to help if and when people ask. We need not be overly anxious about the responsibility. But should we decide it is for us, there are things we need to learn, skills we can acquire, patterns we should emulate. In the final chapter, we will look at the skills we can (and must) learn to be effective.

FOR FURTHER REFLECTION

• Read 1 Thessalonians 2:8. What is Paul saying about the importance of investing our lives in others?

• Write down the most significant spiritual discovery you have made in recent months. Do you know someone who would benefit from its insight? What are some ways you can share it with your friend?

Henri J. M. Nouwen argued that the spiritual helper was not one who has achieved perfection. He used the image of the "wounded healer." A minister, helper, or spiritual friend, in other words, is one who finds the grace to look after the wounds of others, even while he or she continues to be healed.

• Recall a time when someone sought your advice in an area where you have special experience or expertise—from changing a flat tire to dealing with a rebellious child. What did you learn from the experience that might apply to sharing spiritual wisdom?

• Does the thought of talking with someone about the spiritual life frighten you? How much of your fear can be chalked up to simple inexperience? How much do you think has to do with not being gifted in giving another counsel? Talk with a friend or spiritual mentor about your feelings, and seek his or her feedback.

• Keep track of when people come to you for help in spiritual matters. Do you dread such encounters or look forward to them? What might your feelings tell you about whether or not you should take on someone as a spiritual partner or protégé?

• Begin regularly praying along these lines: "Lord, I want to be open to those around me who need to know about you. Open doors of opportunity for me to share, and guide my lips when I am called upon to speak about you." When a door opens, be ready.

USED OF GOD

Few biblical characters were used of God as dramatically as Moses. God called him to lead Israel out of their bondage in Egypt (Exod. 3:1-14), perform numerous miracles, and receive nothing less than the Ten Commandments (Exod. 19–23). That was not all. We read in Exodus 33:11 that God "used to speak to Moses face to face, as one speaks to a friend." Moses was nothing short of remarkable, and no one in Israel had known of anyone quite like him.

But all along, in the background, was Joshua. He was Moses' "young assistant," Exodus 33:11 tells us. At one point, he would not leave Moses' tent, where the glory of the Lord appeared as a pillar of cloud and the Lord spoke to Moses. While he trailed behind Moses, lived with him, and saw him face off against the people's idolatry, Joshua must have made mental notes about the demands of leadership and the cost of faithfulness. Then the Lord told Moses he would not see the Promised Land, that his "assistant" Joshua would be the one to lead the people in. "Encourage him, for he is the one who will secure Israel's possession of it," the Lord told Moses (Deut. 1:38). Then, not long before Moses' death, Moses called the people together. He told Joshua in their presence, "Be strong and bold, for you are the one who will go with this people into the land that the Lord has sworn to their ancestors to give them" (Deut. 31:7).

Was Joshua intimidated at the thought of filling Moses' sandals? It is hard to imagine his not being. But his call contained a promise that must have made all the difference. "The Lord who goes before you. . . .will be with you; he will not fail you or forsake you. Do not fear or be dismayed" (Deut. 31:8). ᕼ

TEN

Directions for the Director

Spiritual directors should soberly realize that they themselves are not the chief agent, guide, and mover of souls . . . but that the principal guide is the Holy Spirit.

John of the Cross

The teaching of the wise is a fountain of life, so that one may avoid the snares of death.

Proverbs 13:14

❧

Author Ted Engstrom tells the story about a young man who dropped in to see his pastor. He came to talk about a coworker at his plant whose life was "a mess." "Would you be willing to talk to him, Pastor?" he asked.

"I'll be happy to talk to him," he answered.

The pastor had lunch with the troubled coworker and found him open to the gospel and spiritual matters.

After some weeks, the concerned friend showed up again to visit the pastor. "The man you had lunch with is in dire need again," he reported. "Would you be willing to see him?"

"Then," writes Engstrom, "a light came on in the head of the pastor. He asked the young man, 'How well do you know your coworker?'

"'I know him very, very well. We've worked together for many years. In fact, we ride together to work and eat lunch together nearly every day.'

"Now his idea grew more intense. 'You know,' the pastor said, 'I may be able to see your friend once in a while but you're with him every day—week after week. Wouldn't it be a much better strategy to train you so that you could teach him about Christ?'

"The layman was willing," Engstrom concludes, "to become a mentor to his fellow worker and out of that came good things for Christ and [Christ's] Kingdom."[1]

Perhaps you are ready to take a similar step. Or perhaps later someone will ask you to be a spiritual mentor. What are some of the basics if and when you say yes?

WHEN YOU'RE READY TO MEET

First, consider using an initial meeting or two to explore the relationship. If you are meeting with someone you do not know well, get to know your partner or apprentice. You need to find out areas of strength or weakness. You may assume your partner is ignorant, when in fact there may be great experience or wisdom. And the converse may be true as well: theologically "correct" vocabulary may mask a person who is barely crawling spiritually. Only as you know the person you are meeting with will you give help that hits the mark.

Asking questions that bring clarity may help. Why did he or she come to you? What are his or her spiritual goals? Are they in line with your understanding of the spiritual life? Be clear that you see spiritual mentoring as helping someone grow in his or her relationship with God; it is not primarily counseling, teaching, hearing confession, or providing crisis intervention.

Be clear also that your interest as a helper will probably not be one of friendship in the social sense (unless it is that already). When I served on a church pastoral staff some years ago, a young man in the congregation called me. He wanted, he said through his awkwardness, to get together with me once or twice a week. "I need someone to go bowling with, to talk to about my job, to be an 'official' friend." He asked this despite our rarely having talked before and our apparent lack of things in common. A part of him, I suspect, wanted spiritual guidance, but that somehow got mixed in with his request for friendship. Had he simply asked for spiritual help, I would have gladly said yes. But his expectations were unformed. They would have led to commitments I was not prepared to give. I gently told him no.

WHEN IT'S TIME TO DRAW THE LINE

Be alert to the possible need for drawing boundaries. Be especially clear that spiritual helping is no substitute (though it can be a complement) for in-depth counseling.

My wife and I once became spiritual mentors to a woman I'll call Jeannine, who struggled with fierce anxiety and depression. Against our advice, Jeannine after a while dropped her regular sessions with her psychoanalyst. She suspected that she was looking to us not only to give spiritual guidance but to provide the kind of support her doctor had been giving her. She began asking for more than we had time or ability to give. We came to a painful point where we had to set clear limits. The issue of how accessible you will be may need articulation in some cases.

It is crucial to watch for times you feel "in over your head" as a helper. If your partner is exhibiting aberrant, destructive, or unexplainable behavior; if he or she is severely depressed; if sexual abuse or addictions come into view, you cannot play counselor unless you have proper training. In such cases, professional help is a must. Referring your friend to a clergyperson or helping him or her find a counselor is a mark of compassion and wisdom, not abandonment. Your role as a spiritual guide may, however, remain as important as ever.

ESTABLISHING NEW DEVOTIONAL "HABITS"

You should also discuss a strategy for your partner's growth in prayer. Because the primary purpose of spiritual helping is aiding the deepening of another's relationship with God (expressed in prayer, Bible reading, and other devotional disciplines), many spiritual mentors find it helpful to suggest a "rule" or outline of spiritual disciplines.

Avery Brooke explains that she finds this helpful in two ways. The first lies simply in having a discipline, "as opposed to praying hit or miss in whatever fashion strikes you at the moment." The second relates to honestly reporting how well or poorly you or your partner have kept the planned-on discipline. "In all likelihood," she writes, "one kind of prayer has gone well and another has not. Such discussions are not narrow. The directee's problems in prayer, failures, successes, understandings, and misunderstandings raise many questions. Is the relationship with God an honest one? Does he have a distorted idea of God? Or why does she favor one kind of prayer over another?"[2]

An obvious and simple way to accomplish this is for both partners to work their way through a book on some aspect of the Christian life. Richard J. Foster's *Celebration of Discipline* or *Prayer: Finding the Heart's True Home* would be an excellent example. Or you might suggest a book of the Bible, sections of which could be read each week to form the basis of your discussion, especially if your partner is not well versed in the Bible. Then again, you might work to introduce your partner to new practices, such as keeping a prayer journal, praying regularly in small-group prayer meetings, or keeping a prayer list for intercession.

Whatever the means used, helping your partner with new habits of prayer and Bible study is not so difficult as it might seem. Most people seeking help for their spiritual life already have some practice established, even if a haphazard one. Chances are they pray at night before going to bed or say grace at meals, read the Bible or devotional books, or experience corporate prayer in church or at a weekly Bible study. They may simply need someone to help them enlarge their repertoire of devotional practice and provide the accountability that will prompt them to do more.

THE SHAPE OF HELP

As you meet your friend, keep in mind these practical suggestions.

1. Provide clean, uncluttered physical surroundings. Your meeting place should generally not be a dingy cellar or cluttered room, or a noisy public place (such as a crowded restaurant). If you meet in an office, consider taking your phone off the hook (or turning on an answering machine) and putting a "Do Not Disturb" sign on the door.

2. Begin with prayer. Not only is God's guidance indispensable to the enterprise, praying with your partner can provide valuable centering and focusing as you both begin.

3. Have a specified time of meeting. For a one-on-one arrangement, an hour is probably enough. Margaret Guenther suggests, "An hour is sufficient; after that, the conversation tends to become repetitive and trivialized. (I make an exception for [those] who travel from a considerable distance and whom I see less frequently.)"[3] A relationship of mutual mentoring where both are sharing may make a bit more time appropriate.

4. Be alert to the feelings beneath the spoken words or outer expressions. Learn to read the soul of another, to listen with what someone calls, "love's third ear." Watch for clues about a person's feelings beyond the words. Be ready to raise questions about the spiritual dimensions of what may initially seem mundane concerns. Be aware that sometimes people do not share their deepest

issues right away. Indeed, in my meetings with
Kevin, we moved into deeper honesty as the years
passed. As you meet, it may take time for trust to
develop before a partner reveals deepest doubts,
admits darker temptations and sins, or feels free to
share cherished dreams.

5. Consider the role of church people in your partner's life. If he or she avoids active participation in
church and other small groups, consider ways to
help the person initiate or reestablish a relationship to a body of believers. Spiritual mentoring is
no substitute for the regular nurture and challenge
that comes from a body of believers. Indeed, the
church provides the wider context of accountability that helps keep spiritual partnerships healthy.
"Not neglecting to meet together" is the counsel of
scripture (Heb. 10:25). Your involvement will be
much more fruitful if your partner's needs for fellowship, worship, and instruction are being
appropriately met through a congregation.

6. Be sensitive to ways you can help your friend
or apprentice cultivate the fruit of the
Spirit—aspects of character such as love, joy,
peace, patience, kindness, and self-control. A
related task has to do with helping him or her
find his or her "spiritual gifts," as Paul calls our
unique, Spirit-endowed abilities. A healthy
Christian life involves generous giving and service to others; spiritual guidance is a very
appropriate setting for exploring the shape of
such expressions of Christian life.

7. Suggest resources to the one you help. Books
by devotional "greats," such as Thomas á Kempis,
Teresa of Avila, Oswald Chambers, or Richard J.
Foster can be a wonderful complement to your
insights, strengthening a person's grasp of the

spiritual life. Keeping a journal may also be a helpful practice for the one you meet with, especially as he or she explores aspects of vocation and direction for the future. The events, questions, prayers, and insights recorded in a journal during the days between your meetings might provide grist for enlightening discussions.

THINGS NEVER TO FORGET

Even more important than such specifics are a couple of broader points to remember as you consider having a hand in influencing another's life.

First, what happens as we meet with another is dependent not only on what we say and do but also on who we are and *whose* we are. Having wisdom that comes from opening our lives to the Spirit will mean far more than being able to answer every question about biblical interpretations or techniques of praying. That should be an encouragement when we cannot know everything and make mistakes (as everyone does).

Sometimes, in fact, it's the forgotten words or unselfconscious acts that matter most. More than once I have heard a pastor, teacher, or youth worker say that the aspects of their ministries that made the greatest imprint have to do not with impressive programs or presentations but with intangibles: how they simply lived what they believed, for example.

For all the ways we can sharpen listening skills and learn about God and human nature, then, transformation comes from beyond ourselves. Someone I know talks about spiritual companionship as "God filtered through a person."

I once talked with a young woman, who, while in high school, saw her life forever changed through the influence of one woman. My friend recalls, "She got me involved in a weekly Bible study." While the woman taught the Bible, says my friend, "I saw how God had changed her life, had made a difference. I saw her personal relationship with

Christ. Being with her and the others in the group, seeing their commitment, helped me to strengthen my own." Now that Margie is an adult, she says, "I see myself in a similar role for others. I see God using me to touch the lives of others in the same way he used this woman to influence me."

A second thing to remember is that our help should not and cannot come at the expense of our own spiritual life. We must not so expend ourselves in the lives of others that we crowd out margins for our own prayer, our own seeking of the Lord's face, our own Bible study. We need to remember that the beginning of wisdom is the fear of the Lord, not a frantic rush to help anyone who crosses our paths.

We need to remember that the beginning of wisdom is the fear of the Lord, not a frantic rush to help anyone who crosses our paths.

Said Bernard of Clairvaux, "If then you are wise, you will show yourself rather as a reservoir than as a canal. For a canal spreads abroad water as it receives it, but a reservoir waits until it is filled before overflowing, and thus communicates, without loss to itself, its superabundant water. In the Church at the present day, we have many canals, few reservoirs."[4] It is an overflowing life in the Spirit that makes us able.

A close family member of mine I'll call Nancy recently met with a dear young woman with immense problems.

The woman grew up in the home of an alcoholic father, and now she has an abusive husband. Nancy realizes that her young friend is very vulnerable and that her needs are great. Nancy knows that God must be the ultimate orchestrator of their sometimes emotionally intense discussions. When they begin their weekly meeting, Nancy told me, she prays out loud for the Holy Spirit to guide them into truth. "Then I try to stay close to God the entire time we're together." And God is so active in healing Nancy's friend that Nancy sometimes thinks her most important role is simply to point out God at work and get out of the way.

No one—least of all Nancy—expects an overnight disappearance of her friend's emotional damage. There will probably be years of healing ahead. But I also know that as two women meet weekly—sometimes with their toddlers clamoring and fighting over toys strewn across the living room floor—the outcome will have spiritual, even eternal, significance.

As that kind of helping takes place through us—and, through others, within us—we will likely be astounded by the joys of companionship. We will wonder how we and those we love ever did without such a relationship. Whatever forms spiritual guidance takes for us in years ahead, our lives will be incomparably richer for the help we gain and give.

FOR FURTHER REFLECTION

• What is your own outline or plan for daily prayer and devotional times? On a piece of paper, outline your typical prayer time. What are you doing that could help someone who needs guidance in how to pray?

• Make a list of three devotional disciplines that need strengthening in your own life, practices that will allow you to be a more spiritually sensitive mentor or friend. Perhaps you need to read more about ways to pray, or you need to be more regular at Bible study. For each of the three, take a separate sheet of paper and outline specific steps that will help you toward your goal. Commit your plans of action to God in prayer and prepare to grow—for your sake, and others.

• Consider a time when someone has asked too much of you, overstepping appropriate demands on your time and energy. How did you deal with their unrealistic expectations? What did you learn that might help you set limits as a spiritual helper now?

• What does it mean that sometimes we help the most by not meddling and letting another's growth take its own course?

• Do you agree that "what we share with others . . . should not and cannot come at the expense of our own spiritual life. We must not so expend ourselves in the lives of others that we crowd out margins for our own prayer"? How do you think you might keep in balance the need to pray with the call to serve others?

A FRIENDSHIP STRONGER THAN DEATH

Perhaps no biblical friendship is more fabled than that of Jonathan and David. Their deep, lifelong loyalty is a remarkable example of how God can use friends to support us and keep us from harm.

Their relationship receives first mention in 1 Samuel 18:1. Jonathan, son of Saul, met David soon after David killed the Philistine Goliath. Jonathan, the prince, "was bound to the soul of David, and Jonathan loved him as his own soul." Saul also opened his arms (and his house) to the young David, inviting him to live with the royal family. But almost from the beginning, Saul began to look at the young, capable, charismatic David with "a jealous eye" (1 Sam. 18:9, NIV). Before long, Saul was scheming to kill him.

Jonathan repeatedly saved David's life, helping his friend escape or elude capture. But he also buoyed David's spirit and offered spiritual reinforcement as David sought to be faithful to God's call. "David was in the Wilderness of Ziph at Horesh," 1 Samuel 23:15-16 tells us, "when he learned that Saul had come out to seek his life. Saul's son Jonathan set out and came to David at Horesh; there he strengthened his hand through the Lord."

We see the depth of their support and love when Jonathan is killed alongside his father in battle. David cried, "I am distressed for you, my brother Jonathan, greatly beloved were you to me. . . . How the mighty have fallen!" (2 Sam. 1:26-27) ᴇ❦

EPILOGUE

When You Can't Find a Spiritual Partner

My friend Paul was brought up in an intensely religious environment. But for all the emphasis on Bible, church, and moral living, what praying he did, he recalls, was "slipshod, shallow, and rarely more than an occasional 'God help me out of this jam!'"

Then Paul discovered the books of Helmut Thielicke, a German pastor and theologian renowned for his application of Jesus' teachings to modern people's desperate problems. Thielicke's sermons, prepared for people struggling through the devastation of Europe after World War II, made Paul aware of the emptiness of his praying. He began to pray about his praying, asking God to help him uncover a deeper relationship.

"The most amazing thing happened then," Paul recalls. Within a week after praying that prayer, he found himself awakened in the early morning hours—morning after morning. After several times, Paul recalls, "It dawned on me that maybe the Lord was answering my prayer. I got out of bed, went to my study, wrapped in a blanket, knelt at the couch, and said, 'Lord, I think this is your doing.'" It was the beginning of a decades-long habit of early-morning prayer. Paul's experience of God was immeasurably changed.

When we can't find a real-life friend or mentor (or even when we can), authors can fulfill the same function, at least in part. Like my friend Paul, authors have at different times immeasurably enriched my practice and understanding of prayer. Richard J. Foster, Eugene H. Peterson, Thomas á Kempis, Augustine, and others have all had an impact on me. Thomas Merton, who combined a calling to prayer with a desire to write, has been an especially meaningful mentor to me, even though I was but a boy when he died. Paul Stanley and Robert Clinton call this "passive mentoring." Stanley notes,

> George Müller [the nineteenth-century British pastor and orphanage founder] is one particular model who has mentored me. One of my goals is to reread him on a yearly basis though I don't always make it. I wish you could see my copy of *George Müller of Bristol*. It's marked all over. Each time I reread it I add more notes. Those notes are values, principles, insights into situations, or suggested applications to things I am now facing. George Müller lived over one hundred years ago. But as I reread his biography and review his commitments and decisions, his life continues to mentor me.[1]

The same can be said of radio and TV programs. I still remember how, in my last year of seminary, my wife and I would find our hour-long commute to school made lighter every day by listening to Christian radio. Especially meaningful to us was the "Chapel of the Air," which challenged us to take our commitment to Christ seriously in daily ways. There can be a consistency in a regular speaker or program that stretches our faith and makes us think of things we might forget.

We may also find a substitute for the flesh-and-blood presence of a real mentor through "long-distance" mentoring. Letters have historically been significant sources of sharing wisdom and insight, as found, for example, by the twentieth-century spiritual writer Evelyn Underhill and her mentor Baron Friedrich von Hügel. My friend Kevin tells me of a time when he would call an old college friend, even though they were separated by thousands of miles. "If I was facing something painful or spiritually confusing, I would pick up the phone and dial California," he said. "I did it only once or twice a year, just when I really needed it. And it helped." People with whom we used to be close, from whom we once derived real strength, can be sources for our ongoing spiritual growth.

The point, of course, is that God can reach us and help us grow through any number of means. That God will not leave us stranded, without means for growth, is a promise of scripture—one we can count on. ⟋⟍

ENDNOTES

CHAPTER 1

1. John Donne, *Meditation XVII.*
2. Richard J. Foster, *Celebration of Discipline* (San Francisco: Harper & Row, 1988), 185.
3. David Mains and Steve Bell, *Two Are Better Than One* (Portland, Ore.: Multnomah Press, 1991).
4. Eugene Peterson, *Working the Angles* (Grand Rapids, Mich.: Wm. B. Eerdmans, 1987), 109–110.

CHAPTER 2

1. Baron Friedrich von Hügel, *Essays and Addresses on the Philosophy of Religion*, quoted in *Writings on Spiritual Direction*, ed. Jerome M. Neufelder and Mary C. Coelho (New York: The Seabury Press, 1982), 8.
2. Aelred of Rievaulx, *Spiritual Friendship* (Kalamazoo, Mich.: Cistercian Publications, 1974), 71–72.
3. Frederick Buechner, *Now and Then* (San Francisco: Harper & Row, 1983), 87.
4. James W. Pennebaker, *Opening Up* (New York: Avon Books, 1990), 14.
5. Paul D. Stanley and J. Robert Clinton, *Connecting* (Colorado Springs, Colo.: NavPress, 1992), 26.
6. Robert Wilkin, "The Lives of the Saints and the Pursuit of Virtue," *First Things*, December 1990, 45.
7. Ben Campbell Johnson, *To Pray God's Will* (Philadelphia: The Westminster Press, 1987), 78–79.
8. William Blake, *A Vision of the Last Judgement, Descriptive Catalogue*, 1810.
9. Alan Jones, in the preface to Margaret Guenther, *Holy Listening* (Cambridge, Mass.: Cowley, 1992), ix.

CHAPTER 3

1. Roger Steer, *George Müller: Delighted in God!* (Carol Stream, Ill.: Harold Shaw Publishers, 1979).
2. Dietrich Bonhoeffer, *Life Together* (New York: Harper & Row, 1954), 97–98.
3. Eugene H. Peterson, "The Summer of My Discontent," *Christianity Today*, January 15, 1990, 30.
4. Margaret Guenther, *Holy Listening* (Cambridge, Mass.: Cowley, 1992), 24.
5. Richard J. Foster, *Celebration of Discipline* (San Francisco: Harper & Row, 1988), 186.

CHAPTER 4

1. Tilden Edwards, *Spiritiual Friend* (New York: Paulist Press, 1980), 107.
2. Daniel J. Levinson (with Charlotte N. Darrow, Edward B. Klein, Maria H. Levinson, Braxton McKee), *The Seasons of a Man's Life* (New York: Ballantine Books, 1978), 27.
3. Barry A Woodbridge, *A Guidebook for Spiritual Friends* (Nashville, Tenn.: Upper Room Books, 1985), 39.

CHAPTER 5

1. David Mains and Steve Bell, *Two Are Better than One* (Portland Ore.: Multnomah, 1992), 19.
2. Richard J. Foster, "Hearing God's Voice and Obeying His Word," an interview with Richard Foster and Henri J. M. Nouwen, *Leadership*, Winter 1982, 19.
3. Ben Campbell Johnson, *To Pray God's Will* (Philadelphia: The Westminster Press, 1987), 82–83.
4. Margaret Guenther, *Holy Listening* (Cambridge, Mass.: Cowley, 1992), 12.

CHAPTER 6

1. Paul D. Stanley and J. Robert Clinton, *Connecting* (Colorado Springs, Colo.: NavPress, 1992), 205.
2. Gary Downing, "Accountability that Makes Sense," *Leadership*, Spring 1988, 42.
3. Tilden Edwards, *Spiritual Friend* (New York: Paulist Press, 1980), 111.
4. Thomas Merton, *The Ascent to Truth* (San Diego, Calif.: Harcourt Brace Javanovich, 1951, 1979), 185.
5. George H. Gallup, Jr., and Timothy Jones, *The Saints among Us* (Harrisburg, Penn.: Morehouse Publishing, 1992).
6. Brother Lawrence, *The Practice of the Presence of God* (Old Tappan, N.J.: Fleming H. Revell, 1958), 8.
7. James Houston, *The Transforming Friendship* (Batavia, Ill.: Lion, 1989), 283-84.
8. Thomas Merton, *Spiritual Direction and Meditation* (Collegeville, Minn.: The Liturgical Press, 1960), 39.

CHAPTER 7

1. Eugene H. Peterson, "The Summer of My Discontent," *Christianity Today* January 15, 1990, 28.

2. Quoted in Jerome M. Neufelder and Mary C. Coelho, *Writings on Spiritual Direction by Great Christian Masters* (New York: The Seabury Press, 1982), 57.
3. Isabel Anders, *The Faces of Friendship* (Cambridge, Mass.: Cowley Publications, 1992), 99.
4. Quoted in Neufelder, 56–57.
5. Paul D. Stanley and J. Robert Clinton, *Connecting* (Colorado Springs, Colo.: NavPress, 1992), 208.
6. Quoted in Neufelder, 36–37.

CHAPTER 8

1. J. D. Salinger, *Catcher in the Rye* (New York: Signet Books, 1945, 1946, 1951), 171.
2. "Hearing God's Voice and Obeying His Word," an interview with Richard J. Foster and Henri J. M. Nouwen, *Leadership*, Winter 1982, 21.
3. Paul D. Stanley and J. Robert Clinton, *Connecting* (Colorado Springs, CO: NavPress, 1992), 175–76.
4. Josef Sudbrack, *Spiritual Guidance* (New York: Paulist Press, 1983), 21.

CHAPTER 9

1. Avery Brooke, *Finding God in the World* (San Francisco: Harper & Row, 1989), 49.

CHAPTER 10

1. Ted Engstrom, *The Fine Art of Mentoring* (Brentwood, TN: Wolgemuth and Hyatt, 1989), 22-23.
2. Avery Brooke, *Finding God in the World* (San Francisco: Harper & Row, 1989), 79.
3. Margaret Guenther, *Holy Listening* (Cambridge, Mass.: Cowley Publications, 1992), 22.
4. Bernard of Clairvaux, quoted in Richard J. Foster, *Prayer* (San Francisco: HarperSanFrancisco, 1992), 168.

EPILOGUE

1. Paul D. Stanley and J. Robert Clinton, *Connecting* (Colorado Springs, Colo.: NavPress, 1992), 148.

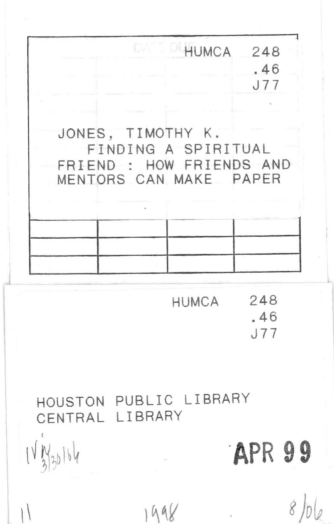